Imagery Treatment for Trauma:
healing addiction, grief, and pain through spiritual imagery

Jared Rockwood, LCSW

ISBN: 9798710756867

Printed in the United States of America

Printed and Distributed by KDP

Dedication: to all those that give their lives in the service of relieving the suffering of others

TABLE OF CONTENTS

CONVERSION

The Guru Metaphor

Traditionally in the East young people would spend their developmental years studying under the same teacher. These teachers were known as gurus. The gurus would nurture their pupils from the time they were young until they were prepared to enter life as adults. They would be educated in language, mathematics, history, and politics. They would learn about human nature and the impulses that govern humanity. They would develop an understanding of themselves, and they would learn about others. The great gurus would not only educate but they would train the future leaders of the nations.

It is said that one of these teachers had developed a ceremony for his graduates. It was the last lesson that they would receive before being sent into the world. The nature of the test was a deeply guarded secret. The final test took place atop a tall mountain, and although many rumors circulated as to the nature of the test, no one knew for sure what transpired there.

The guru and his initiates would hike for days up the side of the biggest mountain in the region. The hike was strenuous and at times treacherous. Eventually the initiate and guru would arrive at their destination, the mouth of a cave. At that time, the guru would give the pupil a bag with a back strap. He would provide some dried fruit and nuts, jerky, and water. He would then instruct the initiate on the expectations of the final test.

My son/daughter, as that is what he called all his pupils, "the task I am inviting you to perform will not be easy. I believe in you, and I know that this final lesson will be the most important lesson you can learn. I want you to enter this cave. This cave snakes along the inside of the mountain until it comes out the other side. In the darkness of the cave, the floor is riddled with rocks. Each time you kick or stumble on one I want you to pick it up and put it in your bag. Be faithful on your trek, and put each rock in the bag regardless of how heavy or cumbersome.

As the pupil entered the cave the darkness quickly became oppressive. The air was stale and dank. Initially there were very few rocks to worry about. After a time, the ground was covered in pebbles. The journey was frustrating because the floor was so thick with these pebbles that kicking them was a common occurrence. Most students initially were diligent and mindful of the instructions, and they began to collect the small rocks.

The darkness was so intense that it was almost palpable. With this oppressive darkness came surges of fear, and at times feelings of hopelessness would wash over the initiates as they traveled through the cave. Time was impossible to track in the darkness of the cave. As muscles began to ach and the bag became increasingly heavy, thoughts would flash through the mind. Inevitably thoughts would include the idea of retreating back the direction they entered. Sometimes the idea of picking up the pebbles seemed so ludicrous. Others would think: "Honestly what is the point of this? Guru must be confused, and his mind has become addled. No one will ever know if I do not pick up every rock. I will just say I walked carefully and pick up only a few as I go." Sometimes they would think that they had a full bag and they had done good enough. The thought of dropping the bag and running away would nag at the mind constantly.

The trek through the mountain was a journey of one to two days for the diligent. Not everyone made it out with a bag. Some would have collected a few pebbles during the journey but were far from consistent in retaining all the rocks they had kicked. Some were fairly diligent and had a heavy load but certainly were selective in what they chose to bring with them. Some of the pupils filled their bags to overflowing and then filled their pockets.

As each student emerged from the darkness of the cave the guru would be waiting. He would embrace each, and he would say, "I love you; thank you." The pupil would hang onto him relieved to have emerged from the darkness and warmed by the guru's love.

Following the warm embrace, the students found that the rocks they recovered contained diamonds. Those who diligently followed the guru's instructions were immediately wealthy. Many regretted shirking the instructions. However, regardless of each student's yield, all were equally loved by the guru.

Awakening

Dr. Gary Weaver, one of my early clinical mentors, used to tell this story to teenagers preparing for an internal journey of self-reflection as part of a therapeutic experience. The first time I heard this story I had just spent several days trekking through a series of slot canyons in the deserts of south-central Utah. I was working at a residential treatment center for youth who had committed sexual offenses. My coworker Gary was preparing a group of boys to participate in an activity he called "solos." The river at this specific juncture had several bends in immediate succession, and there were little oases carved out of the desert; these oases provided solitude and protection from inclement weather, yet each location was within shouting distance of the attending staff. The boys would each spend the better part of two days and an entire night alone, tucked away in an alcove.

I began working with the residential treatment center eight months previously. I worked with a group of twelve boys as lead therapist providing individual, family and group therapy for each of them. Once a week an older gentleman named Dr. Gary Weaver would run a skills group with the boys. This gave me an opportunity to catch up on paper work, prepare for sessions, and provide training to staffs; while he occupied the boys in a productive activity. Up until the day I sat in a circle listening to the story of the Guru I had very limited contact with Gary.

Conversion

When I first started working at the treatment center, I had been told by my superior to steer clear of Gary because he had spent too much time by himself in the desert and was a bit crazy. As a result of the warning I had never taken the time to get to know him personally. All I knew is that he looked a bit out of shape and perhaps a little old to be hanging out with a bunch of young teenagers in the middle of the desert.

After trekking into the wilderness with these young men, we arrived at Gary's basecamp. Gary had not hiked in with us over the last few days but had taken a short cut to the base camp while we had worked our way to this point. Gary set the stage for the solo experience and then dictated where each boy should be placed along the winds in the river bank. Once the boys were placed in their solo spots there was a few hours where staffs just hung out socializing while Gary took a nap, using a round volcanic rock as his pillow. Following his nap Gary indicated that he was going to go out and meet with boys and stated he would start on the lower wing. I had not received any instructions as to my role at this time, but being a therapist, I decided to head out and meet with my boys for some therapy sessions.

As I started meeting with my boys in therapy I was overcome by the powerful conversations and the emotional depth that we were able to reach. Therapy had been transformed into an engaging and emotionally connective experience that surpassed even the best of sessions I had experienced over my previous four years working as a therapist. I decided that it must have something to do with the hiking and breaking down the body and mind through our physical exertion and high adventure experiences we had over the previous few days.

Eventually I crossed the threshold from the boys I had done sessions with to the boys that Gary had met with. When

Conversion

I started working with these boys, a miraculous thing happened. The meaningful and deep therapy that I was coming to expect in this setting took on an almost surreal connectivity. It had an intensity like I had never known was possible. Boys were bearing their soul and talking about personal and meaningful things in vulnerable open ways.

To be clear, I was working with adolescent males with history of sexual offenses. They had created chaos and a wake of pain in their families. And here we were, in the middle of a desert, working through shame and trauma in productive and meaningful ways. I have come to call this cross-over experience "walking in the wake of Gary."

I tend to be the most comfortable in the world of books, ideas, and theory, and I am often a bit emotionally detached. I tended to be scattered-brained and easily distracted, but I like rules and boundaries and predictability (perhaps to compensate for my natural bend towards disorganization). Being aware of my own intuition and spontaneously following my own thoughts unguided by a clear goal and intention is uncomfortable for me. Up until now logic ruled supreme in my world. Emotion did not have a significant impact on me. Tears or anger did not influence or change my thinking; only a well formulated logical argument could really begin to shift my perspective.

B. Wilder

One of the experiences on that trip had a significant and long-lasting impact on me. It was with a boy we are going to call B. Wilder (for bewildered). He was an incredibly smart young man (which attribute was backed up by psychological testing that put him intellectually two standard deviations above the mean), was a bit socially awkward, and was prone to presenting himself as all-knowing. He came from a divorced family where both parents had remarried. He came into treatment after sexually abusing his half-sister on his father's side. The event was so traumatizing to his father and stepmom that they cut off B. Wilder from the family. For all intensive purposes, he had been disowned.

One of the common steps for boys in the program was to complete a sexual history polygraph exam. A polygraph is a tool for assessing the credibility of information presented in therapy, and is sometimes called a lie detector. Prior to the wilderness outing, B. Wilder had failed three sexual history polygraph exams. It seemed very likely that he had sexually touched his sister from his mom's second marriage. B. Wilder adamantly denied having ever engaged in the behavior. To me, this was a logical defense position because of his fear of being disowned by his mom (as had happened with his father) and thus being left all alone in the world. His mom was a loving and supportive individual who wanted to believe B. Wilder. I had stepped in as the voice of logic and advocated for his mom to not close her eyes to the polygraph results. Polygraph is not a perfect science, but our gut instincts on truth and deception is roughly as accurate as the flip of a coin.

This had been a hard and intransigent conflict with the family and the boy. After many discussions, mom had conceded that B. Wilder had likely failed the polygraph because he was being dishonest. I had been trying to help B. Wilder feel safe enough to divulge the missing pieces in an attempt to help him have a firm foundation for building his safety plan (steps to ameliorate risk and support safety in the home and community) and in order to identify people he may have hurt so that they could heal through appropriate intervention.

Conversion

In the Utah desert, B. Wilder had taken seriously the invitation to explore the diamonds of his own mind. When I came upon him to visit he was tucked away in an alcove. As I walked into the alcove he was occupying and requested the opportunity to do therapy with him, an intense feeling of peace and love flooded my body. To be clear, this was without having seen or communicated with B. Wilder in any way whatsoever since the solo began. This intensity of emotion is not something that I had ever felt before, and it was so strong that it felt like I had crossed a threshold into a holy space.

I have told friends the only comparison I can make is to Moses as he approached the burning bush and was told to remove his sandals because he was entering holy ground. There was a serenity and calm about B. Wilder that I had never seen in him during the seven months we had worked together. With his permission, I joined him sitting on the ground, and we began to talk.

He was fascinated by the experience that he had with Gary only a little while previous. When I asked him what he had done with Gary, B. Wilder stated they had done guided imagery, and that he had never felt so much love in his entire life. Being personally intrigued by the odd sensation I was experiencing and the demeanor of B. Wilder, I asked him to tell me what they had done in greater detail. He told me that Gary had asked him to close his eyes and imagine a group of people that had his best interest at heart. Then when that group had assembled in his mind's eye, he was to ask them, "Do you love me? And feel the response?"

I inquired as to who had shown up in his mind. He stated that the most vivid picture was that of his mom and step dad, although there were several others that he mentioned. B.Wilder and I had been wrestling with the issue of the failed polygraph and the hurt and pain that was created in his overt silence. Being a therapist, I have a fundamental belief that the only way to work through an issue is to go through it and experience it fully (versus hide from it or pretend it does not exist), so I took this moment to reach out and grab the exposed nerve that had stifled progress up until this point—not in a malicious or mean way, but by way of invitation to be real.

B. Wilder was aware that I was convinced he was holding onto something more. With the peace and openness that I saw in him at this time, I felt there may never be a better time to get to the truth. I invited him to think about why he was choosing to hurt the people that love him most with his failure to be honest.

In that moment he looked at me and with no defensiveness or irritation he stated, "Jared, I honestly don't know how I am failing the polygraph. I have talked about everything I have ever done. Honest." At that moment a wave of emotion flooded my body, and I felt a tear begin to trickle down my cheek. It was a strangely foreign experience for me. At that moment I believed him. I had no doubt in my mind that he was telling me the truth. Contrary to the logic and facts on the ground, I was confident that B. Wilder was not trying to manipulate, pull the wool over, or con; he was speaking his truth. Having this "conversion" experience, I told him what I was feeling and apologized for doubting him.

Days prior to the camping trip, B. Wilder's parents and I had discussed the research on denial: research indicates that denial is not a predictor of recidivism (engaging sexual misconduct following treatment) and that, although it feels counterintuitive, failure to be honest and disclose does not mean that he could not get better. We had determined that it was time to have him move forward in his treatment. To strike a balance and not allow B. Wilder to feel that he had won, he was invited to include in each of his formal group assignments the phrase "Although I believe that I have been honest, my body says that I have not." In that way, we could deal both with the denial and at the same time be given a pathway forward.

After listening to B. Wilder, I felt an intense moral dilemma emerge within myself. There was an agreed upon pathway forward in his treatment, and nothing warranted a change. The only difference was that I had a fundamentally different belief about what was going on. It crossed my mind that we could move forward without discussing the specific nuances of my belief with the family. I felt embarrassed about my change in position regarding this situation because there was no proof or logical reason that supported that B. Wilder was being honest.

Upon returning from the experience, I decided that it was my ethical obligation to articulate my change of heart to the family, especially because I had worked so hard to help his mom come around to the "reality" of the lies B. Wilder was hiding behind. The call was uncomfortable for me. I described the experience and let them know that I did not need them to believe me but that I felt compelled to be honest about this odd moment B. Wilder and I shared in the middle of a Utah desert.

Although my heart had changed, logic still required we address the failed polygraph. We completed treatment in the same way we had discussed prior to the "conversion" described. He went on to university following his stay at the treatment center. It has been many years since this event transpired, and periodically B. Wilder still checks in and updates me on his life. He has done quite well and is living up to his potential. Neither of us have ever been the same since we shared that moment together.

Summary

There are times in life when we are invited to enter an oppressively dark cavern. In those moments of fear, confusion, and vulnerability, we have a choice to make. Will I pick up the stones that I am kicking along my way? Do I pick up some of them or all of them? Is the weight and burden even worth the effort? Should I just quit and find my way out?

After walking in the wake of Gary, a diamond I pulled from my mine was that there is more than one way to perceive reality. Logic and the mind are powerful and should not be neglected, but there is information that is communicated at other levels. At times these other levels can be deep and profound. These experiences involve an awareness of a full body sensation. It feels like a "conversion" of the spirit. It felt like my mind was kicking against the knowledge that the universe had distilled upon my soul.

I also learned that change and healing do not always have to be a slow and tedious battle of reshaping cognition and behavioral patterns. Sometimes healing and change come in a dramatic wave. It is like a reboot that purges the person of shame, pain, and bitterness. Knowing that healing can at times come in a burst of soul-healing reshaped my belief in what was possible in working with and healing the emptiness and trauma of my clients.

I remember leaving the Utah desert experience feeling bewildered. My soul was stirred in a way I had never experienced before, and I yearned to learn the healing ways that I had witnessed in the lives of the boys we had dragged out into the desert. Even after all these years and many experiences that have transpired, memories of this event reinforce my belief in the system Gary advocated—even if I still feel self-conscious and a bit crazy as I talk about it.

Conversion

It took me almost three months to work up the courage to ask Gary to teach me about what he was doing with the guided imagery work. Looking back my hesitance seems humorous because Gary wanted nothing more than to share what he had learned and to pass on the information. For the next three years, Gary would supervise me once a week where he would teach me principles and share stories of experiences he had using guided imagery. Guided imagery is a therapeutic technique where someone uses their imagination to create an internal (ideally healing) experience through following prompts provided by the therapist to focus the mind.

At times when I felt stuck with a client, we would pull the boy in and work with him during supervision. This would often get them moving in the direction of healing once again. There were many times that Gary directly engage me in guided imagery. Ironically, I was a difficult understudy because although I believed in the process and was using the techniques in my practice, I had not really connected with it the way I witnessed in my clients. I would find myself overanalyzing the process, and I would get lost in my head without being able to feel with my heart.

Sometimes I have to remember my "diamonds." These insights become a support to my moving forward in an unfamiliar wilderness. I always need to keep in mind who has my best interest at heart, because that is when I feel loved, whole, and secure.

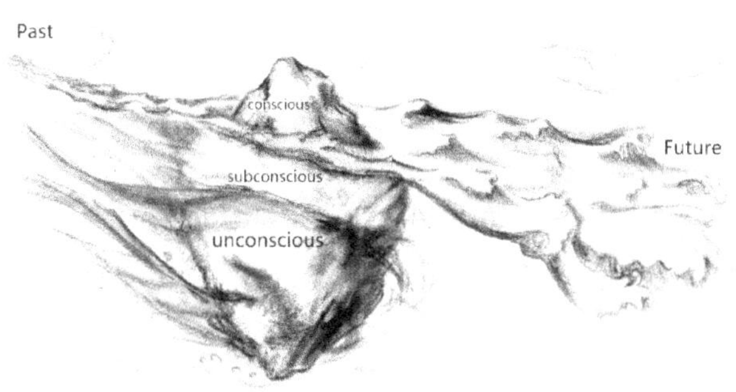

CONTEXT

Maintain Vision

By nature I tend to think in terms of structure, steps, and specifics. I like to know theory, the underpinnings of ideas, and how ideas relate to one another. Dr. Gary Weaver would often laugh as I would try to connect things he said with things I had learned in other venues. There seemed to always be a struggle between us; where I would try to understand themes and templates, he would push me to think beyond the form, to the function.

Let me illustrate this with the story of Moses and the people of Israel from the Bible. They had miraculously fled the captivity of the Egyptians, but they then found themselves wandering for decades in the desert wilderness known today as the Middle East. Traveling with an entire nation of Israel would have been a serious task. People would have been of all ages, physical capacities, and abilities. Indeed, this must have been a major undertaking. Because of the scarcity of food and the magnitude of their group, they would have been completely incapable of survival without Divine intervention.

Eventually the people became disillusioned and confused as to why they would flee slavery to die in the desert wastelands that they were traveling. They had been repeatedly attacked and harassed by the nations they were trying to occupy. At this point in their travels they had tried to send some spies out to find a safe route through unfriendly territory. The scouts that had been sent out were captured and killed. My guess is that the Israelites felt a foreboding about their ability to ever find safety in a land that they could claim as their own. After wandering around for so long it probably felt like the inevitable end to this unpleasant journey would be that they would be picked off and killed little by little until they were wiped off the face of the earth.

This precarious position led many to complain against God and Moses. As punishment for their negative thoughts and disposition, they fell into close proximity with poisonous snakes that would frequently bite the people. Many were dying from these venomous snake bites, and the people eventually turned to God for help.

At that point, Moses built a bronze replica of a snake and placed it on top of a large staff. The people were told they could be healed if they would only look upon this symbol. One interesting side note to this story is the subtle message embedded in the use of a serpent. In Hebrew letters have numerical equivalents, and words with the same value can have parallel or dual meanings. In this case the interesting equivalent is the word Serpent and Messiah. Serpent (Nacash=358) can be translated "to subtly whisper, or learn by experience." Messiah (Mashiach=358) can be translated "spiritual awakening." The people that had the faith to look upon the serpent were healed. These were they who were willing to aligned once again with God.

Almost 700 years later, King Hezekiah reformed the Israelite nation both politically and religiously. He had humbled himself before God and sought out the prophet Isaiah as a confidant and advisor. To regain favor with God, Hezekiah destroyed all the pagan idols throughout the nation. The bronze serpent from Moses era had become an idol of sorts that the people worshiped, and so it too was destroyed. The question is, why would Hezekiah destroy such an ancient and important relic? It seems a shame to erase the symbols of Israel's past in some fundamentalist fervor. According to the story, destroying the bronze serpent was necessary to foster the purification of the people.

This story provides an analogy for the tension that Gary and I experienced in the tug and pull of clarification and routinization of the practice of guided imagery. For years I was able to have weekly supervision under Dr. Weaver's tutelage, and yet his concepts remained somewhat undefined and vague. I would be told over and over again that guided imagery is not about "getting it up in my head but feeling it in my heart." He would tell me the process of learning was not in the memorization or development of specific steps; it was something a person does and experiences. The only way to learn is to do.

Carl Jung once said that in his opinion most churches become a barrier to people's ability to connect with God. This is counterintuitive because religion exists to facilitate the communion of humanity with a Higher Power. There are rituals and forms that can be incredibly healing and connective. However, religion can become a tedious list of dos and don'ts that fosters guilt and alienates feelings from the Divine. What was once a saving staff with a bronze serpent can become an idol—in other words, a hollow ritual lacking power and connectivity to God. I think that part of powerful imagery is the ability to be in the moment, engage the cosmic tumblers of shared symbolism, and believe that healing is going to happen.

Once I finally got it, I would find myself trying to explain these concepts to others but on many occasions where the words escaped me. Often, I would get frustrated and simply say to the person, "Close your eyes. Now imagine a group of people that have your best interest at heart." Then things would take on a life of their own. I have found that sometimes the best meditation is simply working through the initial steps of connecting people to the concepts of guided imagery and then giving them space to work it out from there.

The last thing we should do is put post-materialist guided imagery up on a pedestal, flaunt it as system superior to all other techniques, and then charge colossal amounts of money to certify people in it. The idea is not to create an idol that should be worshiped, but to provide a spiritual awakening to a deeper space of healing. It is not about systematizing a hollow shell of interesting ideas, but co-creating an experience of healing and transcendence that mark a shift in patterns of thought and behavior.

Clinical Fathers

Theory can help guide our thinking and bring us to a place of understanding and acceptance, and it can become an obstruction if we become overly rigid and formulaic. The theoretical arguments that I will lay out here are my attempts to make sense of the magic that I witnessed with clients. I want to be transparent about the fact that these experiences were happening and existed outside an overtly structured and specific theoretical framework. Gary was indifferent about why or how it worked; he only knew that it did. I was so fascinated by the positive outcomes of what I was witnessing that I actively worked out in my mind how and why I thought healing was the outcome to the loving intervention of guided imagery.

I would like to talk about post-materialist guided imagery in terms of some of the founding fathers of the therapeutic movement. I will be focusing on specific segments of the complex belief systems that these great minds brought to the table; and so, therefore, recognize the limitations and oversimplification of some important and complex themes. That being stated, I find it important to look at this work in terms of the broader theory of psychology, theorists, and practice.

We will start by looking at the father of modern therapy, Sigmund Freud. Then we will look at Carl Jung, who happens to be one of Gary's favorite people to quote. And finally I would like to tie in the most recent evolution in my own thinking regarding how this specific form of imagery is embedded in the principles of Attachment Theory as established by Bowlby, among others.

Freud & Jung

Sigmund Freud and Carl Jung were inquisitive and expansive thinkers around the turn of the 20th century. This duo generated some of the greatest thinking in early psychology and shaped the flow of both profession and popular of psychology ever since. Freud has been greatly criticized for extracting entire theories based on relatively limited information supplied to him by highly emotionally unstable clients. That stated, anyone who has experienced psychoanalysis and free association can attest to the liberating and fascinating twists and turns of self-discovery that help to redefine our understanding of who we are and why we behave in specific patterns. Freud was highly sensitive to the interactions between people and how these interactions shape memory and thoughts. He also identified patterns of thinking that we use to keep our sense of identity and well-being intact.

One iconic image that has become indelibly connected to the idea of our internal world is the iceberg metaphor. Freud recognized that many of our behaviors seem to be driven from a force within us that is not directly linked to logic. Although we can adapt behavior based on information and cost benefit analysis, many behaviors seem to be more nuanced and complex than simple logic. The idea is that deep within our minds, we are driven to engage in patterns of behaviors that surpass logic and are embedded in a more primal, raw, and unconscious reality. We have a deep and unseen inner world that shapes and taints our conscious behavior.

Freud would argue that virtually all behaviors we engage in are the byproduct of this intra-psychic world. He understood the world to be fiercely individualistic. We encounter the world and make sense of it in our conscious mind despite the fact that much of what drives our feelings, behaviors, and thoughts is outside of our conscious awareness. He was among the first clinicians to embrace the ideas that we can heal by working through our thoughts verbally and that healing often comes through the interconnection of ideas and shifting of paradigms.

These fundamentals have remained at the heart of therapeutic practice ever since. Different models may take a different stance on the level of interaction, how to shape the discussion, and the role of attachment; yet fundamentally Freud made a transition away from hypnosis into what is now the traditional practice of talk therapy.

Jung was a contemporary of Freud, and they carried on close association for half a dozen years. Freud seemed to look upon the young up-and-coming Jung as a potential successor to his ideology and someone that could carry the work forward. It has been stated that the first time they met they were so enthralled in conversation that they did not break, rest, or part for thirteen hours straight. There was a rupture in their relationship as Jung began to expand and advance additional layers to the initial iceberg theory of unconscious that had been advocated by Freud.

One of the fundamental differences in world views between Freud and Jung was spirituality, religion, and forces beyond the individual. Freud had found inspiration in the ideas and philosophies of Nietzsche who was famous for stating, "God is dead." Freud viewed the concept of God as a projection from the individual for a desire to have an all-powerful father figure to watch over and protect the individual. Jung on the other hand had a fascination with religious thoughts and studied both Eastern and Western traditions extensively.

Jung concluded that at the heart of religious experience was the synthesizing of our internal selves with the Divine. This synthesis reinforced his belief in the process of individual healing as the byproduct of integration into one great whole. He believed we needed to embrace our darkness and our light equally. In so doing we are better able to accept these polarized parts in others. Spirituality to Jung was another layer of this integration of our mortal, imperfect forms and our divine, eternal forms. He believed that religion was not a detriment and opiate to the masses but a necessary element of personal fulfillment and happiness.

Being a pantheist, Jung did not believe there was one pathway to achieve this. There was not one correct system of doctrines and beliefs, only potential pathways to connecting our primal natural selves with our divine interconnected self. This in part interrelates with his fundamental schism with Freud. Jung began to propagate an idea that became central to his thinking about humanity called the collective unconscious. The collective unconscious he believed to be an inherited psychic link to our ancestors and all of humanity. He compared the transmission of physical characteristics and genes with the interconnection of humanity and our collective psychological experience. Jung concluded that this inherited source of wisdom was able to inspire and provide support to the individuation process. In other words, it is in the best interest of collective humanity for individuals to be happy, engaged, and connected. These connections are interpersonal and intrapersonal in nature.

I would like to illustrate this idea of the collective unconscious with a personal story. I have always been an avid reader, and I love books that explore history, religion, and philosophy. I once came across the autobiography of Saint Patrick. As I read the book, called *Confessions* (Skinner, 1998), I had this unreal connection to him and the story. I was not reading this as a religious exploration but as a matter of interest in an ancient historical text. Repeatedly as I read, I found myself feeling caught up and swept away with intense feelings of connection and admiration. I always found this to be peculiar, but it left an indelible impression on my mind and an affinity for the Irish people and culture.

Years later I was reading Jung's *Man and His Symbols* (Jung, 1964). I had been exposed to the ideas of collective unconscious many times, but this time as I read, I had a visceral recall of this earlier reading of Saint Patrick's *Confessions*. It was like the flame of a candle had appeared inside me, and I connected deeply with the idea that my soul yearned to learn of my roots and my people. I come from the Irish O'Carroll line on my maternal side. This overwhelming emotional connection to Saint Patrick was a direct physiological reaction to the fact that Saint Patrick had loved and served my people. He had risked life and limb for my ancestors. To this day, although I cannot prove it, I believe it is very likely that I have a direct descendent that was taught, converted, and brought to a sense of peace and happiness through Patrick. As a result, my body rejoices in his story and in his name.

Bowlby & Attachment

Bowlby brought a new and interesting perspective to the world of psychology. Arguably his early development shaped some of his emphasis on the importance of warm caregivers, thus laying the foundations for overall wellbeing and interpersonal connection. He had been raised in an era where society feared spoiling a child through connection, so his parents were distant and cold (as was the custom of that time). He was raised by a loving nanny that met his developmental needs. At a young age, about seven years old, he was placed in a private school for his studies.

After becoming a therapist, he developed a keen interest in youth, children, and infants. Some of his early work in therapy was focused on adolescent delinquent boys. As he worked with these young men, he came to believe that their early life experiences and connection to caregivers was instrumental in their pathological development. He talked about these young men as putting on a face of callousness and indifference, yet this veneer was only to hide their overwhelming desperation and fear of being hurt by others.

Through the efforts and brilliance of this great man, the entire field of medicine has come to approach the needs of children in a much more healing and productive way. Children that have physical contact with their caregivers survive at much higher rates than those that are kept in sterile, safe environments without human contact.

This reminds me of the Harlow experiments with rhesus monkeys (Harlow H. F., 1965). He provided young infant rhesus with two artificial mothers. One was a wire frame that held the bottle and thus provided the substance of life for these little guys. The other was a frame coated in a soft material that was pleasant to the touch. The expectations were that monkeys would favor the wire mother because feeding is necessary for life. Contrary to these expectations, the mother that was cuddly and warm was overwhelmingly the preferable mother. This was yet more support for the idea that attachment is not just a convenience or a pleasant byproduct of proximity, but it is an innate need for survival. We learn to see ourselves and to see others—not just physically but emotionally, socially, and spiritually—for who we truly are through our interactions with others. The monkeys that lacked the give-and-take and nurturance of a loving caretaker later developed into adults that failed to develop the ability to problem solve, understand social cues, or engage in appropriate self-care.

Let me highlight this further with another social experiment that has two layers we can explore. This time the targets of the studies were human infants and their mothers. Tronick designed an experiment to measure the effects of disrupting the healthy interaction between mother and child, that is, the vocalizations, pointing, and prattle that goes on between the infant and mom. In this experiment, the mothers were instructed to engage with their child for some time but then show a neutral face and cease to respond to the child's bids for attention (Tronick, 1975).

During the first stage of disengagement, a child would increase the positive signs of engagement. The infant would point, laugh, vocalize, and attempt to reengage the mother. When this does not work, a second phase of child responses set in: the child would become fussy, wine, and complain. The clear signs of distress increased. This agitation and fussiness would give way into full-blown tantrum. During the third phase, the child would be in crisis mode. The infant's breathing became unregulated, and would almost turn purple as they protested. The child kicked, screamed, and fought with all their might. What were they fighting for? Survival.

Humans are dependent on their caregivers for longer periods of time than any other species. We cannot survive without our clan, our group, our family. This is not just a fight for attention; it is a fight for life itself. Most depictions of the study stop at this point. It is fascinating to watch the minute the mother begins to engage in attuned interaction, the child is able to regulate, calm, and reengage. There is virtually no hesitation in returning to play and connection. But there is a fourth stage. If the still faces went on for long enough, the child fell into despondence. They stopped fighting. They gave up. There came a time when the child believed that no one could help them.

These stages are mirrored in youth and adults that surround us. Some of us feel disconnected, so we joke around, show off, and entertain. Some of us are so hurt that we grumble, whine, and find little that is positive in the world. Others are lashing out at themselves and others. And a select few have given up, disengaged, and checked out. They are no longer playing the game of life because they have come to believe that no one cares. We are neurologically wired to need others. Not just as infants, but throughout our lives. Self-regulation is certainly highly sought after skill, but the core strategy for effective emotional soothing is co-regulation. It is not about me; it is about we.

Let me add one additional layer to the Tronick still-face study. Siegal and Hartzell in their seminal work *Parenting from the Inside Out* (Siegel, 2003) cite an additional twist to this original study. They talk about a replicative study that mirrors the original, but this time the children and mothers were in different rooms. Each had a video screen where they can see, and therefore interact with the other. In the beginning, the child and mother were attuned to one another, and all the interactive elements were present and good. Instead of Tronick's still-face variable, it was replaced by a feedback loop recording of the appropriate interactions that the child was actively responding to and enjoying just moments earlier. The infants monitor switched from interacting with the mother to the prerecorded loop of their earlier interaction. The mothers were looking behind themselves as if the children were pointing, and the mothers verbally responded with the appropriate prattle. All the fixings for a loving caring interaction were present. But the interaction was not a reaction to the child, so something had changed.

What were the infants' reactions to this scripted, recorded loving caring interaction? Initially the child increases the pointing and vocalizations and positive signs of engagement. When met by a continuation of old interactions without the attuned give-and-take, the children became irritable and began to cry and protest. This initial protest grew into panic. The study did not push things past this point, but we could guess where things were headed. At some point, the children would no longer try to reconnect and engage. They would give up. They would come to believe that there is no hope. How painful life can be when any of us give up hope.

Gary & Imagery

I have developed an image in my mind of how Dr. Gary Weaver's thoughts connected with those early fathers of psychology. Initially there is the person—fiercely independent, like an iceberg, and the person is driven by both conscious and unconscious needs. But similar to Jung, Gary believed that we are not alone. Gary fully believed in the interconnection of humanity, the inherited psyche of mankind. If we think of the iceberg flowing along a large river, it gives us a sense for what Freud's and Jung's ideas look like in combination. The problem with that analogy is that Jung believed that the collective unconscious was inherited (like eye color, shape of ones nose, etc.), so the river would encompass the history of mankind. But in that thinking there is no river beyond the iceberg of the individual.

Gary adds a layer to this image with the river of the collective unconscious not only receiving the past but extending into the future. He believed that collective humanity is not conditional to the same linear time that we think of in terms of past and future. There is a sense of omnipresence. All time existing simultaneously. Therefore, when we are engaging in post-materialist imagery work, we have five resources that can be tapped to aid and foster healing.

    1. we each have unique strengths and qualities; the healing resources in the unconscious that can be drawn from to enrich and support healing (Freud)

2. the collective unconscious that links us together in a common history and struggle for survival, including our personal ancestors and historical figures of significance (Jung)
3. loved ones, such as family, friends, teachers, and coaches (Bowlby)
4. those that will come after the person in the river of time that is yet to be experienced, including a future partner, future unborn children, future great grandchildren, or other figures of significance that are yet to come (Gary)
5. a Higher Power, such as spirituality, nature, collective humanity, or whatever that might look like for us (Jung/Gary)

We will explore these concepts further, but for now suffice it to say that we are not alone. When the battle ceases to be *my* battle against addiction to drugs, alcohol, sex, gambling, anorexia, or gaming, when it stops being *my* fight against depression, anxiety, or bipolar, and when it is no longer *me* against the world, I can refocus and fight the good fight with an army. I am the **captain** of my own future. I am **supported** by those that came before. I am **joined** by those that have loved and cared for me throughout my life. I am **sustained** by those that will follow after me in the future. And I am **yoked** with the Divine. In this paradigm, the impossible becomes possible.

One of the core concepts that we (the clinician or helping professional) must hold onto, once we believe that guided imagery can be a tool to help heal, is that we are not the agent of change. This is a process that takes place between the person who is suffering or seeking insight and their Higher Power. It is a spiritual confluence that acts as a catalyst for change. It is not about the therapist but about the universe and the collective desire for the happiness of the person.

Synchronicity is at the core of powerful imagery experiences. Often the biggest chore is to get out of the way so that the healing can take place despite our involvement, as opposed to because of our engagement. There is some shaping on our part as to the way the imagery emerges, yet when done correctly it frequently takes off in a direction that one had never have intended, planned, or imagined.

YOUR BEST INTEREST AT HEART

Muck Analogy

Namiste (na-ma-stay) is a Sanskrit term that literally means "I bow to you" but is commonly believed to mean "the divine in me recognizes the divine in you." It is worth noting that this is now used as a greeting this is more generic and less formal, but anciently it had these other more spiritual overtones. I have always loved this term as it seems to communicate a deep respect and love that boarders on the sacred. The following is an analogy based on the muck that gets in the way of Namiste.

One way of looking at the divine spark would be that before creation and this life as we know it, there was an essence that existed. This intelligence or light existed before we were born and will continue on following the disillusionment of this temporary tabernacle that we call "me." What is released after this life is the god within, the divine light. This light returns to the timeless eternal and pure state from which it came.

When this light falls from an incorruptible and perfect place into this life, it is like falling into a massive pile of muck. Consciousness and self-awareness develop slowly over many years, and by the time this awareness comes to fruition, the only thing it knows and can see is the muck that covers itself and everyone else. You see, the standard practice in this mortal transient existence is to adorn and venerate the muck that is all around. People wake in the morning and look in the mirror and they fail to see the divine they once were because all they see is muck. When they look around them, they do not recognize Namiste in others, but see only muck.

Not knowing any better, we revel and put value in muck. We give muck to others, and we collect muck for ourselves. We rub it on our faces and all over our bodies. When we care about others, we don't know any better, so we attempt to help them by giving them muck and helping them cover themselves. This creates a very stinky situation.

But sometimes, for brief moments, we may catch a glimpse of the divine in someone else. Have you ever had that experience where you meet someone for the first time, and there seems to be a goodness that radiates from them? Or perhaps (and even better) it is someone that you know intimately and have had the opportunity to spend extensive time with? Such as a parent, grandparent, coach, teacher, dance instructor, or the like. You are drawn to them in an inexplicable way, and you yearn to get in touch with that radiance in yourself. This is the birth of Namiste in you, and if you are lucky, it will grow and develop until you are able to see past the muck and into the divine in yourself and others. If you have this blessed opportunity, the external becomes irrelevant as the internal light radiates in spite of the muck all around.

Debriefing

The purpose of this analogy is to provide a foundation for talking in a different way about life experiences. In a nutshell, the purpose of therapy is to create a new narrative about experiences and life, a narrative that can support healing and replace of self-loathing, hate, and dysfunction. There are times when I have used this analogy for the purpose of opening a new dialogue about who we are and the relationship we have with others.

The pieces of the story that seem to resonate most with traumatized kids include the piece about life being crappy. Many of them were dealt a horrible hand in the game of life, and that is unfortunately the reality of the situation. It is not fair, it is not rational, and it is not ok. A good friend of mine, a fabulous therapist, was a sergeant in a local jail for most of his career in the public sector. He studied to become a therapist because he thought if he could help high-risk adolescents, perhaps the problems that lead to prison could be resolved before they solidified and became ingrained. He would tell the boys that jail is full of two types of inmates: those who see themselves as only victims and those who take responsibility for their actions. The latter group were the least likely to return to prison. This is purely anecdotal and comes from one sergeant in one jail, so I am not purporting this as an empirical observation. But it was his observation, and it makes sense to me.

My hope and trust in the youth I've done therapy with is often matched with anger and disdain from them. They seem to struggle to see the good in themselves, and therefore any compliment or positive connection is viewed with distrust. Sometimes the muck analogy provides the youth with a small window into why they cannot see Namiste in themselves or others and why all they see is the muck in the mirror. In the case of the boys I am currently working with, they have hurt others in very real ways. These boys shared their muck and gave it to others because the boys did not know what else to do with it. This way of talking about things in a meaningful way that is less shameful than focusing just on the hurt they have caused others. Ultimately it seems to be a true axiom that people who hurt hurt people.

Odie Umh

It is not uncommon for those of us that do therapy to feel our hearts break as a young person describes the horror and trauma that tainted his or her early life experience. One such young man we are going to call Odie Umh. His story is a litany of worst-case scenarios all compounded onto him, his older brother, and younger sister.

Odie was the middle child to a mother who did not know the fathers of her three children. She struggled with serious addiction and, in part, because of economic limitations, she paid for her drugs by selling her body. This situation brought a revolving door of seedy individuals into the home. Odie Umh has limited memory of these early years, but he does remember hiding in the closet with his siblings as his mother was brutalized and violated. He carries immense guilt that he never stopped what was going on, but of course he had no power to protect or to maintain even his own safety. He and his siblings were sexually abused during these early years by multiple unknown assailants.

Eventually he was pulled from his mother's home as Child Protective Services became aware of the situation. He and his siblings were placed into foster care. Initially the sibling set was placed in the same home, but the trauma of their earlier lives played out in inappropriate sexual play, typically orchestrated from the oldest sibling. This involved all three of the children. For their own protection, when it was discovered, they were separated into different foster homes. Odie Umh had gone from losing his mom to losing his siblings. He had a vivid trauma memory of watching a car drive away with his older brother bawling as he reached for Odie. Despite any problems and the sexual orchestrations of the older brother, this boy had served as the one constant nurturing protector to Odie. Now for the first time in his life, he felt completely alone.

Odie settled into the routines of life with his new family. He recognized that despite missing his siblings, he began to feel safe in an environment where there were clear boundaries and rules and where life was predictable. Yet, in a cruel twist of fate, the very home that was employed to help provide safety and healing for this young man eventually recreated the abuse from his early years as the father in the home began to sexually violate Odie.

Odie Umh went through a series of foster homes before being adopted by a couple that had a big heart for a young nine-year-old. Unfortunately, the adoption did not last for long; Odie had developed severe sexual compulsions that made him unsafe for others without constant supervision. After it was discovered that he had sexually abused one of his adopted siblings, he was once again placed outside the home. He lived in a variety of residential treatment centers and proctor homes from the time he was 11 until he aged out of the system. At 18 he moved out on his own without any real financial or emotional support from his adoptive family. His two pillars of support included a therapist from our facility and a pastor that had run a kid facility and provided a home for Odie for a few years when Odie was younger.

I remember being very anxious when Odie moved out of the facility and would be on his own. I had a hard time finding hope in my heart for his future. Despite all the odds, and his past problematic behavior, he has become a successful adult. In his mid-20s now, he has never cycled back through the legal system. He is drug free and living a life that any parent could be proud of. He has found employment that plays to his strengths, and he has chosen a professional path that helps build the confidence and self-esteem of others.

He called to check in and give an update on his life just a few weeks ago. In the conversation, I asked what treatment he felt made the difference in his success. He replied that he became aware of his own value. He decided that he was not broken and destined to failure, but that he was the master of his own destiny. For the first time in his life, he looked in the mirror and could see past the muck. For the first time in his life, he felt like people cared about him unconditionally. When he recognized that other people could see him for who he was, despite his past behaviors, and they had *his best interest at heart*. He began to believe in his own Namiste. Once he felt others had his best interest at heart and recognized his Namiste, he felt like it was important that he mirror this unconditional acceptance of himself, and he began to live with his own best interest at heart.

Fli T

For a time, I was working with adults with substance abuse problems. The typical profile of clients fell along two lines: young adults (19–25) addicted to opiates (opium, pain pills, etc.) or stimulants (methamphetamines, cocaine, etc.) and adults who were alcoholics or were abusing prescription medications. Most of the people that came through the facility were also parents. It was incredibly touching to hear them talk about their commitment to their children and the motivation being a parent gave them to become clean and sober. There was true love in their hearts for their children and a recognition that their behaviors were not only negatively impacting their own lives but that of their children as well.

One such individual we are going to call Fli T. He was in his mid-20s and struggled with an opiate addiction. He had a preteen son that was the beginning and the end for him. Fli T talked about his son frequently with adoration and praise. The boy's mother had chosen to not be a part of his life and she was rarely involved with him. She would check in sporadically but often only with encouragement from Fli. Fli T had held down a job for several years and was generally able to provide for himself and his son. Their living conditions were not fancy, but they were sufficient for their needs. But, after failing a drug screening at work for marijuana, Fli found himself in the unemployment line. Things went from bad to worse as he chased his loss with the succor of heroin. Within a short time, he was using all of the time and ceased to be the loving father that his son needed. With encouragement from his parents, checked himself into inpatient rehab.

Despite having had several unsuccessful treatment stints, Fli T indicated he was fully committed to completing treatment. He was not going to leave early and he was going to do everything he could to put his life back on track. His sincerity was contagious, and he was a real leader with his peers; holding himself and others accountable for their behaviors. He really dug into his emotions around his own childhood trauma when his father overdose and died while sleeping in the same bed with him.

The program was designed to be 60–90 days, but as is the case in most situations, insurance does not dictate treatment dosage by needs. Fli was only given 30 days of treatment through his insurance with another 15 days sponsored by his family. As he was gearing up to leave the program, I remember taking a trip with him to his apartment so we could clean it of all paraphernalia and remanence of his heroin use. He was able to clean up scraps of tinfoil and remove all vestiges of his old using life. We overturned mattresses and cleaned out cabinets and did everything else possible to set him up for success. The combination of his outstanding personal work while in treatment, solid transition plan, and burning love for his son really seemed to be the recipe for success.

Unfortunately, that was optimistic thinking. Within a short period after leaving rehab, Fli T had relapsed and was in full-blown, self-destruction mode, compromising his ability to be an effective father. His love for his son was not enough to stabilize Fli T's broken, addicted brain. He eventually ended his life, leaving scarring trauma on the next generation.

Summary

I have always found the intro question to Dr. Gary Weaver's imagery work to be powerful. He would say, "Imagine a group of people that have your best interest at heart. Ask this group of people, do you love me?" I remember asking my mentor one day why he did not just ask, "Imagine a group of people that love you." His response has forever changed the way I think about the concept of "love" versus "having someone's best interest at heart." Many people love others. They love them sincerely and to the depths of their souls. And yet they are unable to get outside of themselves in such a way that the love translates to good decisions for those they love. Their addictions, relationships, body image issues, pursuits of pleasure, and attempts to escape get in the way of treating others they love in a way that keeps the others best interest at heart.

In the Bible, there is an interesting verse that states, "Can a woman forget her sucking child, that she should not have compassion on the son of her womb?" Being a father of four, my immediate and emphatic response to this question would be absolutely not. The bible verse continues: "Yea, they may forget, yet will I not forget thee" (Isaiah 49:15). In my layman's translation, this means parents absolutely *can* forget their own children. When I look at clients I have worked with over the years, I can see many examples of such. The story of Odie Umh clearly illustrated a mother that forgot her "sucking child." My assumption in the early years of working with adolescents was that this "forgetfulness" was akin to not loving them. In working with adults in treatment, I came to learn that they most emphatically do love their children. These parents just fail to keep the children's best interest at heart.

Having someone's best interest at heart is not just a feeling of affection and attachment (love) but is choosing to put someone else's best interest before your own. People with your best interest at heart are people who love you and look out for you. They are healthy enough to be able to keep balance in their life in such a way that they are emotionally safe and have the energy to help others as a result of their own capacities. Love is not just a feeling, or a statement, but an action. Having someone's best interest at heart is a love that has a visible behavior that manifests in one's life over and over again.

The description I provided is a good way of measuring what it means to *have someone's best interest at heart*, but I would expand this concept far beyond just having someone that shows up for you in your life. I would add a cosmic level to this definition. For many of us, there is a transcendental component to life that acknowledges that this life is a temporary condition on a more eternal plane of progression, not unlike the muck analogy we discussed earlier. When someone is invited to close their eyes and "imagine a group of people that have your best interest at heart," I will often add, "This can be anyone throughout all humanity, alive or dead, known or unknown, anyone that has your best interest at heart."

Let me illustrate this with a story that touched my heart from Elizabeth Gilbert in her book *Eat, Pray, Love* (Gilbert, 2006). She describes a time when she was having a life crisis as her relationship with her husband ended and they were trudging through the divorce process. Legal proceedings were moving along slowly, and there were a lot of hard feelings. Liz did not want to feel so negative and was struggling to figure out what to do with the depleting energy. As she was on a road trip with a friend Iva, Liz described the tension and conflict and just wished it could come to an end. Iva asked her if she had asked the Universe/God for help. After some discussion, Liz wrote a petition for God's help to end the conflict. Then comes my favorite part, Iva then tells Liz to first sign the document in her heart and then to think of others who would sign it. Liz goes through a list of family and friends while Iva periodically adds names of her own. Iva then expands Liz's options: "Anybody can sign this petition, living or dead." A burst of names comes forth including the Clintons, Abraham Lincoln, Gandhi, Mother Teresa, the Dalai Lama, among others.

Liz writes, "The names spilled from me. They didn't stop spilling for almost an hour as we drove across Kansas, and my petition for peace stretched into page after invisible page of supporters. . .   I became filled with a grand sense of protection, surrounded by the collective goodwill of so many mighty souls. The list finally wound down, and my anxiety wound down with it." Soon after, Liz received a phone call from her attorney who said that the divorce papers had finally been signed.

Liz's experience mirrors those of many clients I have worked with over the years. The sense of loneliness and disconnection is closed through the miraculous connectivity of the universe, through our collective humanity, and through a spiritual strength that goes beyond our own. The result is often not just a feeling of security and warmth but positive action that develops through the cosmic tumblers of synchronicity.

When I have trained therapists in this technique, they commonly ask, "What if no one shows up for the client? When they invite someone to show up that has their best interest at heart, if no one shows up, won't that be even more traumatizing?" Let me answer that in two ways. First, someone almost always shows up. Without much effort or preparation, it just happens. Second, if no one shows up spontaneously, I will usually start to construct some possible scenarios. I will ask if there is a parent, grandparent, aunt, uncle, brother, sister, cousin, neighbor, or coach. I will ask if anyone has passed away that the client knows is watching over them. I will even ask the client to imagine future friends, partner, or children. The options are limitless, and somewhere along the line, something will connect for them. It happens almost every time.

On the rare occasions that a client is truly stuck with this first step; we spend some time talking about why he or she is afraid to have people show up. The issue is not that someone is not there for the client; it is that he or she has shut and sealed the door to the assistance of others. These can become incredibly meaningful moments as we process through the client's side of that connectedness equation.

One of the things that sets this type of imagery apart from other methods is there is no reliance on physical senses. I do not ask clients to visualize a beach, feel the sand in their hand, or hear the waves crashing to the shore. I have no problem with that type of imagery work, but the core of guided imagery work I am promoting is attachment: real, meaningful human connection on the soul-to-soul level. Namiste.

Gary, my mentor, was once invited to Columbia University to talk about the imagery work he was doing with the boys in the group home. He presented to the doctoral students and professors, but he also had the opportunity to do some work in a youth homeless shelter associated with the university. These are youth that are on the street, often in the face of total familial alienation. This is a space where it may be hard to imaging clients would readily be able to envision a group of people that have their best interest at heart. And yet they connected. It did not even require the building steps I described previously. It just spontaneously worked. I have found that the anxiety clinicians have that it will not work far exceeds the actual experience of my clients.

Take for example Odie Umh. The core people you expect to be involved in the lives of most people were not involved in his. He did not have his birth parents, foster parents, or adoptive parents. And yet he found connection naturally in the processes, and he felt loved when he asked, "Do you love me?" The deep profound love that he found was overwhelmingly positive.

When I first started using guided imagery I was not quite prepared for the overwhelming visceral feeling that would enter the treatment space as we did these exercises. There are still times that I will be in the middle of a session and have the intuitive tug that we should start guided imagery work, and as soon as we start, I can feel a shift in the room. This shift is sweet; love simultaneously touches the hearts of me and the client. There is nothing better to set the stage for great healing work in treatment than this attached, loving, connecting spirit that comes with this inspired introduction.

There are several therapists that I have trained over the years that will stop at this point, and they don't take the step I will describe in the next chapter. I recognize that there is a leap of faith required to follow this sequence through to the next phase, but I believe that if you chose to sidestep the next phase of the introduction, you also diminish the quality and intensity of the healing power of the intervention. I think this style of imagery can be helpful and healing without pushing things to an overtly spiritual place—as I will promote in the next chapter—but without it, the client's healing process is potentially undermined by the therapist's discomfort with the divine. My invitation is that you experiment with the entire script as it has been designed by Gary. I do not want to dissuade someone from using only the pieces that work for them, but I also want to advocate from the standpoint of the client's healing experience.

HIGHER POWER

Bill W

I want to start this discussion with a story about a few well known individuals whose lives intersected in such a way that the world was changed. Perhaps it was chance, or maybe it was luck, but more likely it was Divine. As has been mentioned previously, Carl Jung was one of the early founders of psychoanalytic therapy and had an overt spiritual component to his thinking. This was very much contrary to general psychology both in his day and in ours.

In the 1930s, Dr. Jung was treating a hopeless alcoholic. The client was a rich and successful businessman. After a series of unsuccessful treatment attempts, this young man traveled to Switzerland to work with the famed Carl Jung. After a year, Dr. Jung decided the plight of this young alcoholic was hopeless and Dr. Jung discharged him from treatment. Dejected, the young man asked if there was nothing more he could do in seeking recovery. Carl told the young man that there was no medical treatment that would help his alcohol problem and then added that the only hope he had was to experience a genuine conversion, a spiritual transformation.

The young man reached out to a religious society known as the Oxford Group which triggered just such a spiritual renewal. His experience touched the life of the man Bill W, who in turn worked with Dr. Bob. Both of these men experienced a spiritually transformative experience where their alcoholism was eradicated through a conversion experience. Many of you will recognize the names of Bill W and Dr. Bob as the founding members of the Alcoholics Anonymous (AA) movement (N/A, 1939).

Alcoholics Anonymous has a very flexible definition of Higher Power, and they even dedicate a chapter in their primary text talking about agnosticism that invites people to keep their minds open about what constitutes a Higher Power. That stated, there was an intriguing exchange between Bill W and Carl Jung in the early 1960s. Bill wrote of his own spiritual conversion that transpired in 1934 while in a detox facility in New York City. Bill had attempted many, many times to achieve sobriety without success. His treating physician believed his drinking would lead to one of three outcomes: death, insanity, or incarceration.

While in the detox program, being aware of the hopelessness of his situation, a deep depression darkened and overwhelmed him. He described himself as being at rock bottom, like he was at the bottom of a pit. In this state of total futility, he cried out to God in agony. Bill remembers pleading desperately for God to reveal himself. Bill promised he would do anything it took to be delivered from his disease. In that moment, his hospital room was flooded with an intense white light. There are no words to describe the ecstasy that washed over him.

Higher Power

Like many prophets of old, he was swept up to the top of a mountain blanketed in a spiritual wind. "Freedom!" became the clarion call of that moment. He felt an internal strength and confidence that he was "healed" from his disease and could successfully embrace a life of sobriety, happiness, and peace. From that day on, Bill W never took another drink. This experience became an anchor in his life that had a two-fold effect: he would return in his mind to this liberating moment by reflecting and reliving the feelings and experience in his mind's eye, and he would strive to help others find liberation through the same light that saved him from his alcoholic void.

In 1935, Bill traveled to Ohio for business. After an unsuccessful bid, he found himself almost penniless and with intense cravings to use alcohol. In order to cope with these feelings, he reached out to a local church inquiring if there was another alcoholic he could help. He was the living embodiment of what would become the last of the steps. Step 12 states, "Having had a spiritual awakening as the result of these steps, we [try] to carry this message to alcoholics, and to practice these principles in all our affairs." Through these efforts, Bill comes to know Dr. Bob and is influential in recreating the healing he had in his own life in that of Dr. Bob's. This team then founded the 12 step program of Alcoholic's Anonymous that has gone on to be a catalyst to healing in the lives of so many others that had been hopelessly lost. Not only has it extended its healing influence to alcoholics, but it has launched movements related to drugs, sex compulsions, relationship problems, food, shopping, gambling, and countless other life-impairing maladies.

Schism between Psychology and Religion

Sigmund Freud is considered to be one of the fathers of psychology. He was a highly controversial innovator in his time and continues to be someone that is both derided and venerated in our day. One example of this would be his initial theories of neurosis that included some of the first published accounts of child sexual abuse. He put forward a theory that an adult's mental health was negatively impacted by the presence of sexual abuse as a child. This assertion was so derided that he pulled back and reformulated his thoughts including concepts such as the oedipal complex (infantile eroticization of parent leading to homicidal feelings that must be repressed).

Modern research, including the adverse childhood experience (ACE) studies, would corroborate Freud's initial insights that there is a significant correlation between early childhood experience and later complications, both psychological and physiological. Risk factors include things like experiencing sexual abuse, witnessing domestic violence, having a parent incarcerated, substance abuse in the family, or emotional abuse, among other factors. A few examples to illustrate the impact of these risk factors could include the following. The presence of any ACE risk factors increases the likelihood of a suicide attempt two to five times, and the presence of six or more risk factors increases the risk for suicide by almost twenty-five times. Adverse childhood experiences increase the risk for substance abuse disorders, tobacco use, and other addictive behaviors. Presence of ACE increases risk of cardiovascular disease, poor dental health, and diabetes. Life expectancy is decreased incrementally in correlation with each added ACE risk factor (Lewis, 2015). There is a great TED talk by Nadine Harris from 2014 that highlights some of these findings (Harris, 2014).

Higher Power

Unfortunately, in acquiescing to the professional pressure to revise his theory of paternal sexual abuse, Freud created a theory about the internal conflict of a child sexualizing his or her parents. These revisions moved the conversation from the actual experience of clients being abused and developing psychological problems to theories that obscured the reality of child sexual abuse, blaming child sexual fantasy in place of allocating the appropriate blame on the offending adult. This abstraction obscured the reality of incestual relations and introduced victim blaming formally into the psychological literature. Thankfully, we now have a more clairvoyant perspective on this and are in the position to help those that are suffering from the psychological scars of such abuse.

Freud also influence modern psychology with his beliefs about God and religion. Greatly influenced by Friedrich Nietzsche, Freud believed that society had evolved beyond the need for the psychological projection of Deity. That may explain, in part, the significant gap between the spiritual beliefs of the masses versus the spiritual perspective of psychologists in general. Research conducted by Delaney, Miller, & Bisono (2007) published an article entitled "Religiosity and spirituality among psychologists": A survey of clinician members of the American Psychological Association" that had some interesting findings comparing religiosity in the general population to psychologists. They pointed out that a Gallup poll that showed 92% of the people surveyed endorsed a belief in God. On the other hand, roughly 50% of psychologists described themselves as atheist with another 11% describing themselves as agnostic. If these samples are representative, it would show that while the vast majority of American's endorse a belief in God and the majority (61%) of practitioners either do not believe in God or believe that such knowledge is unknowable (Delaney, 2007). My purpose is not to encourage psychologists to reconsider their belief in God but to understand that in order to be client centered, practitioners should consider using the spiritual beliefs and resources of clients as a tool for helping them access meaning and healing.

Group Therapy Anecdotes: Indi Structble & Persephone

During my time working with adults in recovery, there was a theme that would periodically emerge in group therapy. This was not a theme suggested or promulgated by me but was the natural outcropping of conversations among group members. Most clients would be in the facility anywhere from 30 to 90 days, 45 being the average. About every 60 days, we would cycle through the theme of God and the protection he provided while our clients were in the throes of their addiction.

The very first time the topic emerged, Indi Structble spoke of a life-threatening accident he was in while under the influence of heroin. At the time, he knew better than to be driving on the road, and he could feel himself nodding off. A friend that was with Indi would yell at him to wake up and pay attention. As they traversed a canyon road, a semi-truck caught a gust of wind and veered towards Indi's sedan. He panicked and overcorrected pulling sharply at the wheel. All he remembers was his car spinning and rolling.

The freeway that day was not crowded, but there were vehicles surrounding him. He remembers the car skidding to a stop on its hood while he was hanging upside down. Neither he nor the passenger was killed or seriously hurt, and none of the other vehicles on the road were struck. Indi remembers having a strong impression at the time that his protecting angels had saved his life and protected others from injury. As Indi Structble told this story in group, there were tears in his eyes. His story sparked an intense discussion, and many other group members shared their stories of God's protection.

There was a young woman, we will call Persephone, who told her story of leaving treatment prematurely and feeling an intense shame that she was unable to set her life straight. One of the risks that opiate addicts are subjected to as they leave treatment is the dynamic of relapsing while their bodies are not acclimated to the doses they were using prior to treatment. A high dose that their bodies could historically tolerate could now kill them after a period of sobriety. This is a reality for many struggling to find recovery. Persephone, together with her treatment center roommate, checked herself out of residential care because the experience was overwhelming and she was unable/unwilling to live with the restrictions and supervision required in the group home.

After leaving, Persephone and her roommate hooked up with a few friends to get heroin. As she prepared the dose, she could hear the voice of her therapist in her mind warning her of the risks of relapse after a period of sobriety. Her internal sense of shame for leaving treatment and her hopelessness drove her to intentionally overdose hoping to escape the pain and suffering of her life. When she came to, after overdosing, she was somewhat disappointed to be alive. Her bunkmate on the other hand was not so lucky and had used for the last time. Persephone had a complicated concoction of emotions that included intense survivor's guilt, feeling like she should have died as opposed to her friend; at the same time, she could feel a spiritual awareness that there was something more to her life than just fading out in the throes of a heroin overdose. Persephone immediately checked herself back into treatment to finish what she had started, and she felt like God had saved her so that she could help other addicts that were without hope.

The stories poured out of the clients in group therapy. Each connecting with the experience of the others. The theme was consistently a sense that they did not feel worthy. They were willfully putting themselves in high risk situations where they or others may end up dead. Despite all of this, God loved them. He was watching over and protecting them, and He wanted them to find peace, happiness, and healing. This style of group discussion would periodically reemerge (every 2–3 months) with a seemingly universal experience from virtually all group members of God's hand in their lives at the darkest moments of their addictions.

Bill W believed that this "white light" could not only make for a connecting and powerful group discussion but could become the foundation of a complete renovation of body. Where the vices that oppressed the mind and body could be shed and eradicated, not through the strength and worthiness of the individual, but through the power of the Divine.

Nobel SuFring

I want to share a story about a young man that we are going to call Nobel SuFring. Before I set the stage for the story, I want to start with the disclaimer (as opposed to ending with it). I don't want you to think as I share this story that the intention or goal of the imagery work is to convert someone to the idea of a Higher Power. We are not to convince or impose the idea of a Higher Power. But, a client gaining a belief in a Higher Power can be an unintentional byproduct of the healing experience at times. With that background, I will launch into the experience.

Higher Power

Nobel was a very intelligent sixteen-year-old male that was placed in residential care because he had sexually abused his younger sister. One of the complicating components to Nobel SuFring's situation was his intensive history of hospitalization for depression. He had been hospitalized just shy of a dozen times over almost a decade. When he was only seven years old, he was hospitalized for a suicide attempt. Darkness and hopelessness were two of his closest friends.

Nobel was extremely intelligent. His IQ fell around 134 making his score in the second standard deviation from the mean, or in other words, less than 2% of the population. He would use his own intellectual capacity to control others perception of him. He would avoid working on core treatment issues through distracting treating professionals with less threatening outside issues.

His initial transition into residential treatment was very difficult. He was upset that his parents had made this choice for him and he did not have any control or say in the decision. He went on strike for the first 4–6 weeks of treatment. Nobel would not participate in any activities, group work, or peer interactions. He would often lay outside on the grass for hours on end being watched over by staff. Slowly he started to settle in and do some of the work. His emotions became less volatile and he was able to connect with others, first to adults, such as line staff and therapist, and eventually to his peers.

Once Nobel SuFring was settled into the therapeutic flow, he was able to do some of the core emotional work around issues of his parents' divorce and his early feelings of abandonment. Both parents remained in his life and both eventually remarried and had additional children reinforcing his sense of exclusion; despite receiving love and support from all of the parental figures involved. The broken inner child came to mistrust adults, others generally, and God specifically. Coming from a family of faith, he had plead to God that his family stay together. He plead for internal safety during years of darkness and turmoil. The logical conclusion from these years of stilted communication with God is that there was no one out there listening to his prayers.

In the early stages of treatment, anytime I engaged him in imagery work I would modify the second stage of the introduction. I would start with the first step asking, "Imagine a group of people with your best interest at heart. Ask them, do you love me?" Then in place of the common second step of asking him to imagine his Higher Power, he was invited to imagine his "higher self," which I defined as the part of him that lived before he was born and continues on after he dies. It represents the very best part of himself. Carl Jung characterized the "Self" in a similar manner describing it as omnipresent and outside the traditional time-space continuum.

Nobel SuFring was very difficult to get close to. He had eyes like daggers that pushed people away, and his emotional instability was unsettling to people. I remember his peers feared to give any type of feedback or make comments about Nobel in group therapy because they were always concerned with his potential response. If he did not like what people said he could become loud and demeaning asserting his own self perceived superiority and making others feel bad about themselves. He could be very vindictive and condescending when he felt challenged or questioned. Nevertheless, Gary took a great interested in this young man with the prickly exterior. Nobel came to have a great respect for Gary and his corky humor and stubborn insistence on caring about Nobel even after receiving more than a few barbs from this young man.

Higher Power

One day Gary and Nobel were talking, and the discussion focused on the last time that Nobel had truly felt happy, safe, protected, and loved. Nobel was pulling up a blank. Gary suggested guided imagery as a tool for memory retrieval. He set up the imagery normally: "Imagine a group of people that have your best interest at heart. Now ask this group of people, do you love me?" Gary then launched into the second layer without the filter of "eternal self" that I had applied previously and asked him, "Now, imagine connecting with God or your Higher Power and ask, do you love me?"

Nobel would later say that it felt like he was transported into an alternate universe. His entire person was flooded with a loving light that was overwhelming. In the imagery work, he worked his way back to the womb as a place where he felt truly happy, protected, and loved. The feeling permeated his being and did not dissipate upon completing the imagery. He described the experience as a switch being flipped, a light being turned on. In one moment, he felt alone, nihilistic, and lost; in the next, he felt existentially linked to God and broader humanity. He felt a compassion and love for others and himself, which feelings had always eluded him.

Nobel SuFring went on to become a disciple of imagery work, encouraging peers that were suffering or feeling lost to reach out for help. If he learned of a peer having a trauma reaction, like a nightmare or anxiety attack, he would drag them to the therapy office, tell them to sit down, and instruct the therapist to help them with imagery work. Nobel dug into his own personal work, and by the time he completed treatment, he was a happier, kinder, and more compassionate human being.

He attributed this change to his experience with Gary. This monumental shift saved his life and set him on a course for personal success and achievement.

Summary

It is understandable that someone may feel uncomfortable with the idea of an overt spiritual component to a therapeutic technique. For the most part, spirituality in therapeutic practice is outside of the traditional training that we may have been exposed to in university. That was no different than my own experience, but once I had experienced the powerful change in the lives of young men that had been touched by Gary's imagery work, I was left with a longing to know how to help facilitate meaningful healing in the lives of my clients. The consistent positive effect broke down any reservation I might have had regarding the use of spiritual imagery in my therapeutic work. My only goal is to support the client's healing process. I recognize that I am not the agent of change, but the client is their own agent of change. I have also come to learn that the client combined with the Divine is the ultimate healing team. I have no power to change or heal my clients. But their Higher Power most definitely does. The Divine's love for us is infinite. And in the white light of Divine Power comes the renovation of the body and soul such that we are a new being.

I am not convinced that a belief in a Higher Power is *required* for healing to transpire, but I have found that it can be a *catalyst* to healing in many clients. In my years working with adolescents with sexual behavior problems, any conversation that included spirituality seemed to be scoffed at by other professionals. Yet I've learned as I've working with addicts, spirituality is widely accepted as a legitimate theme and resource for healing. The mindfulness movement in psychology seems to be one attempt at introducing an overt spiritual practice under an umbrella of mental wellness. At the end of the day, mindfulness is unabashedly borrowing from the ancient wisdom of Eastern spiritual practice in meditation. The imagery work I am advocating is adding a flexible way to borrow from other theistic beliefs as a catalyst to individual healing.

One of the important nuances here is that a clinician must remain client-centered. It is important to approach these interventions with the client's belief system at the center of your approach. I am against people imposing their personal belief system or striving to create a conversion experience. I acknowledged that there have been times that conversion-type experiences have occurred (Nobel SuFring), but they were not intentional or expected.

The component that I overtly advocate is that as clinicians we do not allow our own discomfort with spirituality as part of psychotherapy to impede healing opportunities for our clients. I have trained therapists over the years that shirked taking the plunge into the second layer of the therapeutic framework in this imagery practice. Their results lack a certain healing quality at times; it is not that omitting the Higher Power renders the treatment ineffective, but the treatment did not have the same traction and outcome.

The tightrope we walk in this area is that we want to respect the belief systems and culture of the client while at the same time leaning on spiritual themes that can aid in the healing process. Traditionally the therapeutic work between a client and a therapist has been a dynamic exchange between the therapist and the client. A feedback loop is generated where ideas are shared and explored, and the client's internal resources are supported with reframing and skill development. My invitation is that we completely rethink the relationship in therapy. We allow for a truly client-centered experience where the therapist at times steps out of the equation and the focus becomes the relationship between the client and the Higher Power.

In the following chapters you will notice a theme: silence. One of the most peculiar dynamics involved in this type of therapy is that you set up the imagery using the attachment model of 1) people that have the client's best interest at heart and 2) Higher Power. Then as you move into the actual therapeutic intervention, over and over you will find yourself saying, "Take as long as you need and let me know when you are done." Then you sit in silence as he or she works through the experience in his or her own mind. One of the exciting and fun pieces to see is when someone has slight twitches and movements, you can be assured that they have reached an almost dreamlike state.

The client's experiences are often vivid and memorable. Years after completing treatment, when people reach out and check in with me, they will often reminisce about specific imagery experiences. They can recount them in detail and have intense emotional connection to the experience even years later. The reality is imagery work is probably less than 10% of the therapy I do with a client, but it represents 90% of what they identify as being the changing moments that aided in their healing. In the following chapter, I will give a template to follow for the introduction of imagery work and alternatives that may aid in different situations. Do not be too rigid in your thinking and approach to imagery work. It is important that you listen to your own intuition. There will be internal tugs and spontaneous ideas that enter your mind, teaching you where to guide the intervention. Trust this intuition. It just might be a Divine spark given to you to aid in your clients' healing. This imagery work is intended to be a synthesis of clinical practice with spiritual roots. Trust those roots and have the faith in yourself that you will be able to get out of the way so that your clients can have a healing experience between them and their Divine. We just have the pleasure of witnessing the process.

Post-Materialist Guided Imagery

- Imagine a group of people that has your best interest at heart; they can be alive or dead, known or unknown, real or imagined, anyone throughout all humanity, but they must have this one thing in common: they have your best interest at heart.
- Once they are gathered, I want you to ask this question: Do you *love* me? (pause then add) *Feel* the response!
- Now I want you to imagine that your Higher Power steps out from among this group of people that has your best interest at heart. I want you to connect with that entity, individual, or power; I want you to ask the same question: Do you *love* me? (pause then add) *Feel* the response!

At this point, you can use one of the templates that will be presented in the next chapters or allow the organic process that develops between you and the client guide you to the needed outcome.

INCANTATIONS

Cheshire Cat

    Alice's Adventures in Wonderland was the brainchild of Charles Lutwidge Dodgson (pen name Lewis Carroll) (Carroll, 1865). It was created as entertainment during a river trip for the three daughters a friend of Charles. One of the little girls happened to be named Alice. The story itself is a nonsensical gander as it follows the character Alice after she fell down a hole as she was tracking a talking rabbit. She struggles with themes of self-awareness and acceptance as well as personal empowerment and independence.

Incantations

After almost drowning in her own tears, talking with a hookah-smoking caterpillar, tending to a baby that turns into a pig, and almost being burned out of a house, Alice is overwhelmed, lost, and in need of direction. In her moment of need, there is a classic scene where Alice converses with the Cheshire Cat at a crossroads. It went something like this:
> Alice: "Would you tell me, please, which way I ought to go from here?"
> Cheshire Cat: "That depends a good deal on where you want to get to"
> Alice: "I don't much care were—"
> Cheshire Cat: "Then it doesn't matter which way you go."
> Alice: "—so long as I get *somewhere*"
> Cheshire Cat: "Oh, you're sure to do that if you only walk long enough."

The charm in this interaction is the irony of young Alice asking for directions without knowing where she in fact wanted to go. The cat responds with the stark reality of the situation: for someone without a destination or goal, the direction he or she chooses becomes arbitrary. Eventually Alice wakes and looks back on the many adventures she had experienced as perhaps nothing more than a dream.

Her overarching goal throughout the adventures in Wonderland was likely laced with the desire to find her way back home. The crossroads had a clear solution if Alice could have recognized and clearly articulated her goal. Perhaps the story of Alice and Wonderland would have found a different resolution if she had the goal of finding her way home from the outset.

Flexibility and Intuition

The very first time I tried to teach guided imagery to others was when I was working as the clinical director for a small company. The company ran three group homes for male adolescents with sexual behavior problems. Trauma was a common theme among the adolescents there, and I felt guided imagery would be an important skill for my therapists to develop to help them facilitate meaningful change for these boys.

Most of my experience came from Dr. Gary Weaver, my mentor, and watching him do the work on clients. He and I talked extensively. We set aside an hour a week to train and develop my understanding of imagery. By nature, Gary is not very linear in his thinking, and these conversations had a way of meandering through all sorts of interesting topics. Unfortunately, the conversations did not unroll in such a way that there was a clear path for teaching the themes.

Gary had an obsession with the idea of intuition. He would tell me all the time to just listen to the intuitive tug and follow its lead. I would tell him that I wanted direction and an understanding of principles and theory. He would tell me that I needed to stop thinking and just do it. I would argue that one's competence in implementing practice comes first through knowledge and then through experience, and that is why we attend university before practicing therapy as a clinician. He would flip this on its head saying that you learn through doing, so therefore the knowledge was secondary to the experience; university is for degrees, and it is not until a therapist is practicing therapy that he or she really understand what to do in therapy. And back and forth we would go.

Because this form of imagery work, he advocated, had so many diverse applications, there certainly was something to the idea that knowing a few fundamentals was the only important principle, and with some general guidance, the rest would fall into place. My experience teaching how to do guided imagery over the years has been that practitioners new to guided imagery struggle to implement it without some clear guidance and templates to draw from. Thus far this book has tried to lay down some of the theoretical foundations that I found useful in understanding what was happening. The truth is that the theoretical underpinnings may not be totally necessary to practice and use this form of guided imagery, but because I find it interesting and helpful, I have tried to establish the roots that can grow into a flourishing application (doing) of the themes I have presented.

Most of the remaining chapters will focus on pragmatic application using a variety of potential templates. I need to emphasize the fluid nature of these protocols. These are not rigid and strict rules for success; they are simply guidelines to invite you to practice what is being presented. That stated, the most rigid and strict protocol is simply to create the safe healing space for the therapeutic work by inviting the client to imagine a group of people that has his or her best interested at heart, ask that group of people if they love him or her, and then imagine his or her Higher Power, asking that essence if the client are loved. These represent the roots from which everything else can be placed.

I remember the very first time I was teaching about imagery, I put together a PowerPoint with about ten slides. The emphasis was simply these two steps with some suggestions on the specific wording. I ended my training by telling my clinicians that after inviting clients to imagine their higher powers, the clinicians could "do anything you want," and in the phrase "anything you want," it was imperative that they think of a mystical voice and imagine fingers being wiggled around as if to cast a spell. My therapists were not impressed. Immediately I was bombarded with questions of "how" and "when" and "what." I believe that first go was a total flop, and not one of my therapists even tried to use the technique.

The next time I put a presentation together, I tried to lay down more of a philosophical argument for its use. I laced it with more stories and specific examples to illustrate the utility value and flexibility of the intervention. This time the group seemed to be more interested, and all of them talked about wanting to use imagery.

Ultimately, my goal in training my therapists was not to create a prolonged mentorship prior to implementation; but was that they gain confidence in the conceptual framework and dive into the work (do). In my mind, our clients are suffering, and we do not have time to get to the next conference or learn the newest techniques (although I highly advocate for continuing education to add and enhance your tool set). In the daily grind of the office, theory does not help distressed clients. Action does. At the same time I have been fascinated many times as I have worked with clients. Hearing their stories can bring theories to life. Cycles of abuse, identification with the abuser, trauma recapitulation, and family roles all have played out in the stories I have heard clients tell. Knowing the theory behind each circumstance helps my brain to conceptualize the problem, but theory does not always translate to a solution. My hope is that guided imagery will lead you to pragmatic and straightforward solutions to problems that theory only helps to conceptualize

The evolution of my training regimen has slowly increased the likelihood that conversation and training will translate into direct action. The last piece of the evolution that helped to bring this to full fruition seemed to be the addition of specific templates that a clinician can use in practice. In my trainings, I often have people practice and use the fundamentals of the technique. We do not dive into templates or deeper emotional work, but we simple run through the fundamentals. Let me review that quickly here because repetition is the foundation of learning.

Foundation

When I am introducing imagery to a client, I do so most often with this question: "Do you want to try something weird?" That is pretty much all I do. Way back in the day, I would explain some of the theory and my whole iceberg in the river analogy, but eventually I became aware that was all for me. Spiritual imagery was a technique that was so off the beaten track I was trying to set the stage and gain some legitimacy through explaining the process. Once I realized that was for me and not for my client I stopped doing so much explaining. Now I simply state, "Do you want to try something weird?"

Most clients will consent. Then I tell them to get in a comfortable position. I tell them they can lie on my couch or just sit comfortably. I let them know we are going to be doing some imagery work and that most people prefer their eyes closed but that such is not necessary. If the client closes their eyes, I often close mine as well. This does a few things. On the one hand, it may be awkward if they feel like I am staring at them. If they were to peak or check on what I am doing, it shows them that I am also participating, providing more of an attachment model interaction where I am both saying and doing with them what I am instructing. That is good for bonding and firing up mirror neurons.

Once they are comfortable, I typically will tell them to take a few cleansing breaths. I will instruct them to breathe in, and as I say this, I make an exaggerated noise of sucking in air. Then I tell them to let it out slowly, and I blow audible to show the slow exhale. I repeat this about three to five times. Then I explicitly tell them they do not need to continue breathing in that way throughout the imagery and it was just to help get them into a relaxed place as we get started.

At this point, I launch into the imagery protocol. I start by saying, "Imagine a group or people that have your best interest at heart. They can be alive or dead, known or unknown, anyone throughout all humanity, but they must have this one thing in common: your best interest at heart."

Typically, I leave a small silent gap and then state, "Once they are all gathered in your mind's eye, I want you to let me know. You can do this by giving me a thumbs up, grunt, or whatever; just let me know when you are ready." Then I sit in the silence.

When they give me the indication, I then say, "Now as you are looking at this group of people that have your best interest at heart, I want you to ask them this question: Do you love me? and *feel* the response!" I tend to space each segment of the instructions and emphasize just a touch the word *feel*.

Next, I tell them, "Imagine that from among that group of people that have your best interest at heart steps forward your Higher Power. God, Vishnu, Buddha, Allah, whatever that looks like to you. Now I want you to connect with that power, with that essence. Look them in the eyes and ask the same question: Do you love me? And *feel* the response!"

At this point, I tend to pause for a minute. Sometimes I will add, "I want you to imagine that feeling as a light, and as you breathe in, it fills your entire being and chases out any darkness. Let it fill your toes and feet, legs, torso, arms, and head until it is radiating from your entire being."

Incantations

I do not always add the light component, and I am not sure what specific circumstances warrant the addition, but my intuition guides me to include or exclude it—as your intuition will guide you. There was a time that I would ask questions about where they felt it in their body and how big it was and stuff like that, but I have basically abandoned that as part of my practice. The common and most interesting response was that there was a visceral difference between the connection they felt to loved ones and that of their Higher Power. They would almost universally identify the feeling between them and their loved ones as being in their chest and being large (filling their torso), but the clients would describe the feeling between them and the Divine not as being in their chest but as being all over their bodies and immeasurable. In part I think I stopped asking because the responses were so consistent I did not need to ask. I already knew. Both connections were powerful, and one was more powerful than the other. This was not always the case, but in the vast majority of the people I engaged these questions with the response was the same.

After setting up:

1) Imagine a group of people that have your best interest at heart a) do you love me?

2) Imagine your Higher Power b) do you love me?

3) From there I move into whatever the next step will look like. I pick from one of the many templates or launch into whatever is in my heart and mind at that point.

Templates

The following are some of the specific templates I will review in the next chapters. I will provide here the name and a brief explanation of each. Each chapter will start with a story, a description of the intervention, and then some potential template language (similar to what you saw above). You could certainly skip to the sections that are the most interesting to you, but ultimately I would encourage you to read through all of them at some point to gain a comprehensive understanding of these common situations. I will again emphasize that you can "do whatever you want" in a mystical voice with wiggling fingers like I am casting a spell, but these templates are also helpful. Do not confine yourself to these few options because the utility of guided imagery really is limitless.

- Trauma: The single most common intervention I do with guided imagery is for intense traumatic experiences. Trauma is one of the most common underpinnings for sexual abuse, addiction, and mental health. Because of the prevalence and seriousness of trauma, I start with this template.
- Family Plague: This addresses the intergenerational nature of trauma, addiction, and family dysfunction. The family plague template is a creative way of empowering a client to take control of his or her own life in the face of adversity
- Weak Link/Ego State: There are many applications for ego state therapy, but one way I have used this is to create a "group therapy" setting with the client and his or her various divisions of development, called ego states. These ego states can be chunked by years of life, periods of residence, phases of education or employment, etc. The goal is to identify and strengthen any "weak link" ego states that have compromised development.
- Eternal Self: This is a great, safe way to break up unhelpful thought distortions. The client imagines his

or her eternal, better self and receive advice from that eternal self. This template has the potential to enhance a sense of meaning and provide pragmatic steps for healing that comes from their own internal resources.

- God Shopping: This concept may feel sacrilegious to some, but many people hold dysfunctional concepts of the Divine; these dysfunctional concepts can lead to feelings of abandonment, betrayal, and hurt. In this intervention, the client fires the god that is not working for him or her and replaces it with one that does work for them.

- Grief Work: So often we hear people say they wished they could have had just one more moment to say that one thing that was unresolved. Say they loved the individual, or they were sorry, or tell them off for hurting them. Whatever that is, we facilitate that dialogue in a safe, internal, imagery place.

- Memory: In the work I did with adolescents who had sexually abused others, it was common that they would struggle to talk about details or additional victims. They would claim they do not remember specific experiences or how they got into various stations. Imagery became an easy non-confrontational way to get into those conversations where shame may prevent honesty. In addition it can be used in other situations where memory seems to be an impediment to moving forward in therapy.

Summary

In my first futile attempts to teach guided imagery, after clinicians would learn the basic principles of setting up an imagery, they would ask me, "What way ought we to go?" I would use the mysterious voice, wiggled my fingers, and say, "It doesn't much matter where you go." They would then protest, "But I want to get somewhere."

I hope that the remainder of this book will provide a "somewhere" and that you contemplate on where it is you would want to go with your clients as you do imagery work. I will work through eight specific templates, but there is no reason to limit your creativity to these specific themes. I share the templates because my experience taught me that clinicians with a clear path to follow were much more likely to use the concepts that were being taught.

Even if you are skeptical at this point, I would encourage you to try it out with a client. I became involved in imagery work not because I thought it was a cool or interesting idea. I became involved because I saw clear changes and shifts in my clients when they had the imagery experience. I don't believe imagery work is a panacea of perfection. It will not work every time, and it will not work with every client. But that is expected. To say otherwise would be to deny the individuality and complexity of human nature. In effect, guided imagery is a useful tool to have in your toolbox.

In my practice, actual imagery work probably makes up about 10% of the interventions that I use. That stated, I have found that when clients call to check in years after completing treatment, the themes they remember and want to talk about 90% of the time are related to guided imagery. They don't talk about successfully working through seemingly unimportant decisions or the powerful cognitive shift from identifying and challenging thinking errors. But they do remember feeling loved and connected to the group, staff, and therapists.   And they remember the powerful healing moments that were often connected to imagery experiences.

Incantations

There is something unique and visceral about imagery work. It feels different for the clinician, and it feels different for the client. It feels different because it is different. They remember the experience because it works.

TRAUMA IMAGERY

Immediacy

There are cultures throughout the world that relied on shamans for healing practices. Shaman is a broad term with many different potential meanings, but the fundamentals of shamanistic healing are to use an altered state of consciousness to obtain healing while tapping into the spiritual force for the benefit of people in the here and now. One of the beliefs in shamanic culture is that one's suffering is most often the byproduct of soul fragmentation. In other words, the traumatic experiences of life damage and divides the spirit, body, and mind. Shamans attempt to enter an alternative state of consciousness to interact with the spiritual world and repair or return fragmented souls.

Many of us may have an adverse reaction to this kind of language—soul, spirit, altered consciousness. I am not claiming clinicians should become shamans, but I would suggest that some of the principles that are manifest in the soul-repairing journey are parallel to what we are trying to create in an imagery healing. The alternative consciousness is the imagery, the shaman is the client, the soul-retrieval is the reshaping of the traumatic memory.

Soon after completing my studies, I worked at a local outpatient clinic that worked with an eclectic mix of clients, as is the case in most outpatient settings. The owner of the clinic was also one of my favorite professors at university. He is a brilliant man with lots of energy, intellectual curiosity, and profound insight. I was very blessed to have him as my initial supervisor coming out of school.

Although we worked with a variety of clients of different ages with different needs, the two groups that seemed to be most attracted to the clinic were adolescent boys that had engaged in sexual misconduct (typically around ages twelve to eighteen) and young victims of sexual violence (typically around ages three to fourteen). Working on the two very different sides of this fence was an eye-opening experience. I was never in the position of having to work with the same siblings set where one was victimized and one offended as these were separated among the clinicians in the clinic. But it did put us all in the position of trying to understand and empathize with both sides of the trauma experience, with those that were helplessly subjected to the abuse, and with those that perpetrated the sexual violence.

At that point in my early career, I had completed a narrative-based trauma therapy certification and was using this trauma therapy in my practice. I found myself being very cautious and slow to address the narrative work. I had a lot of fears about opening "Pandora's box" and unleashing an emotional torrent that I would not be able to contain. I remember a good friend of mine talking about how trauma work should be done with caution and only after a significant period of building rapport with a client and buildings the client's self-regulation skills. For many years, this was my approach to therapy. I would put on the "kid gloves" to approach trauma and usually would slowly warm up clients and move into trauma work over time.

Then I met Dr. Gary Weaver. He would take youth out on these week-long therapeutic adventures and there were times he knew little or nothing about the client, and yet he would dive into the most intense abyss of trauma therapy straightway. At the time Gary was doing these wilderness trips once a year and he felt compelled to maximize the experience and he would tell me that Divine synchronicity had placed the client there with him in this healing space, and therefore the preparation was already accomplished. He just had to invite the client to engage in the healing.

For many years, I worked as a clinical director in an adolescent group home. Clients would live at the facility for nine to eighteen months. Although rare, some kids were there for two to three years. In this environment, I did not always feel pressured to do intensive work immediately, and it was not uncommon that my clients and I would work with one another for months before getting into the deeper trauma work. I was not opposed to doing the work earlier if they were having trauma symptoms (invasive thoughts, nightmares, etc.), but typically trauma work was not something we did from the outset.

Then I worked at a drug and alcohol rehabilitation center for adults. In this setting, most clients were only in the program for thirty to sixty days, and it was like a pressure cooker for therapy. Clients came into the program primed to work and desperate for relief from a life that had become uncontrollable. Combining the short program length and earnestness of the clients with the very real risks of client relapse and death after treatment, the luxuries of building rapport and wearing 'kid gloves' became a thing of the past

I hope that I have never been cavalier or reckless in my approach to trauma work, but I have become bold. I believe that if a client presents issues that include trauma, we do trauma work. In rehab, it may literally be a life-and-death decision. One of the symptoms of the trauma is substance abuse (coping), and alleviating the emotional pain connected to those memories could make the difference between life and death.

So, this is what I would do.

Trauma Imagery Template

I usually move into trauma work if something came up in the session. Perhaps the client was talking about a clear trauma manifestation such as a nightmare or flashback involving the trauma. Perhaps the client was discussing a conflict with those around them that seems to have emotional intensity that goes beyond the current situation. In such cases, I might ask a "float back" question such as, "When else have you felt that way? Are there other situations where you remember feeling like this?" Such prompts can probe the neural networks for connections between the present experience with trauma from the past.

When trauma is presented, I will often simply state, "Are you willing to do something a little bit weird?" Often that is the only preparation I give them. If they indicate a willingness I tell them to sit comfortably or to lie down. I let them know that we are going to be doing a guided imagery and I want them to be as comfortable as possible. I often start with a few deep breaths that we do together while their eyes are close and I use exaggerating noise to indicate sucking in air, and slowly releasing it. The idea is that you synchronize yourself physiologically with the client triggering mirror neurons and a sense of connection and attachment.

Then I ask them: "Imagine a group of people that have your best interest at heart. They can be alive or dead, known or unknown, anyone throughout all humanity, but they must have this one common interest… your best interest at heart." "Once they are collected in your mind's eye I want you to give me a thumbs up or a grunt or indicate to me somehow that you can see them or sense them or whatever." Waite until they say they have it, and then I tell them: "now I want you to ask that group of people that has your best interest at heart, Do you love me? And feel the response!"

Once they have a moment to really connect and feel that love I will say: "Imagine that from among this group of people that has your interest at heart steps forward your Higher Power, God, Mother God, Vishnu, Buddha, Allah, Christ, whatever that looks like to you." "I want you to connect with that power, with that essence." "Now I want you to ask the same question, Do you love me? And feel the response!" Sometimes I add a little narrative about chasing out all the dark and filling their body with light. I don't always use that but will sometimes use it to reinforce the idea of completely turning themselves over to that sense of love, peace, and connection.

Then I will instruct the client, "Look back over the group of people that has your best interest at heart, and ask for two volunteers, two people that would be willing to help you work through hard emotional work and support you through this process." I never provide any specific instruction on who should be involved or what types of people should be invited. It is interesting that most clients will select one person that is a loving nurturer and the other person that is a strong protector. I do not see anything wrong with providing direct instruction; but often I like the organic, natural process of whatever ichnography the client identifies; more often than not, it will be the duo of a nurturer and a protector.

I will then tell them, "You can tell me who those two people are if you would like, and I will use their names throughout the imagery. If you prefer, you can just hold onto that information. Do you want to share the names?"

It is not uncommon that people will share the names, but the more criminally involved your client the more likely they are to withhold the information. In terms of the process, it does not matter if the client does or does not tell you his or her volunteers. I have a poor memory, so I will often jot down the names if the client shared such information. Then I tell them, "Ok, this represents your dream team. There is you, your Higher Power, and [identified volunteers]."

Then I tell the client, "Imagine a vehicle of some sort. It can be a car, boat, plane— whatever you want. Once you establish the vehicle that makes sense to you, I want you to get into the vehicle along with your dream team. Then turn to your Higher Power and ask that being to bring you and your dream team back to that event. *But*, before you go there, I want to emphasize a few things. Because this is in your mind's eye, you have a lot of control over what happens. In your mind, you can put things on pause, you can rewind or fast forward, you can make things small, you can make things big, you can make things black and white. your mind is a magical place, so you are not going to relive anything or re-experience the event; you are going to reshape, change, and manipulate the memory of the experience."

With that as the background, I tell them, "Go ahead and have you're Higher Power take you back to the time of the event. You and the dream team will not travel right into the middle of the situation but just outside the home or place of the event, so you are in the space but not in the event. Let me know when you get there."

Once they signal they have gotten to the appointed place in their mind, I tell them, "Now I want you to come up with a plan. You and the dream team are going to work together to set this situation right. What happened to you was not your fault. And it is not fair that it happened. You and the dream team are going to come up with a plan to 'fixing it.' Any of the players can be involved in any way that you want. Once you have a plan—take as long as you want—let me know."

Then I sit in silence and wait for the client to indicate that he or she is ready. Then I simply say, "Ok, go and do the plan. Make it happen. Fix it. Take as long as you want. Let me know when you are done." At this point, there is often a long gap of time where you sit in silence. Don't rush anything or look for a quick resolution. Sometimes you will see autonomic twitches in your client as they work through this. I usually take those as a sign that the client is invested and into whatever is playing it out in his or her mind.

The silence at times can last a good twenty to thirty minutes. Sometimes the client will have tears streaming down his or her face; sometimes the client tenses, and you can see a visceral body experience happening. Often there is a resolution component where you can see the client relaxes his or her shoulders and facial muscles. Sometimes it is more mellow, and you wonder if the client fell asleep, but eventually he or she gives you the thumbs up, speaks, or otherwise let you know that he or she worked through it.

At that point, I always check in about where the perpetrator is located within the client's image. Usually the perpetrator will not be in the scene, but if for whatever reason they are in the frame of experience at that time, I tell the client to gather up his or her dream team and the little them that experienced the trauma and instruct them to leave and to find a peaceful, safe place. Once there is that psychological distance from the perpetrator, I will have the client do a closing ritual. In this closing ritual, I will have the client hug each of the members of the dream team. I tell the client, "Now that you are in this safe place, I just want you to give the little you a big hug. I want you to love that part of yourself. Tell him/her how strong, beautiful, and awesome he/she is. Ask the little you if there is anything he/she want to communicate to you. Take as long as you need. Let me know when you are done."

Once the client has connected with that little self, then move on to one of the helpers that accompanied the client during the exercise. If you know any names, pick one by name and say something to the effect of, "Now I want you to give [identified volunteers] a big hug. I want you to feel their arms around you, and I want you to feel their love for you. As you are giving them a hug, I want you to just whisper in their ear anything you would want to tell them, anything you want them to know. Then listen to what they have to say to you. Take as long as you want. Let me know when you're done."

Let them work through that ritual with the first helper, then with the second, and then with the client's Higher Power. "Now I want you to give a big hug to your Higher Power, and feel the love. Within this embrace I want you to tell them anything you need them to know. Then listen to what your Higher Power has to say to you. Take as long as you want. Let me know when you're done." Finally, I tell the client, "When you are ready, I want you to come back into this space and open your eyes."

Once the client opened his or her eyes, I usually will ask if he or she is ok. Then I say, "You do not have to talk about any of the details, but do you want to process your experience further?" Sometimes the client will want to talk about it, and sometimes not. There are times the client will launch into a huge description of the experience, and there are times he or she will tell you little pieces without describing the entire process.

I will confess that I love it when clients want to tell me about their experience, but I do not push for it, and I take a very soft approach to the debriefing. It is not uncommon that clients will just say something like, "That was really weird," or even, "What was that?"

When I contrast this type of therapy to other forms of trauma therapy I've used, imagery work seems to consistently give clients a greater sense of resolution and containment. I don't remember an instance where the imagery work itself triggered a client in a way that wasn't manageable. Usually guided imagery seems to create closure that allows clients to functionally move on from the session and sometimes trauma symptomology such as nightmares, panic attacks, ruminations improve or resolve.

Most my career I worked in residential care, so I was not limited to fifty-minute hour sessions with clients. That has always had huge advantages; I have often been towards the end of a fifty-minute hour session when I felt strongly we should do trauma imagery work, and because there is no obligation to be done at a specific time in that setting, I would launch into the work. I have done trauma imageries that lasted twenty minutes, and I have done some that lasted more than two hours. Clearly that would create challenges in more traditional outpatient clinics. I cannot speak with confidence about how to ensure it can be completed and contained within a single session. I would assume in those time-sensitive situations, you would not want to start the imagery late into the fifty-minute hour but instead introduce the idea of imagery and let the client know that imagery will potentially be the focus of the next session. Then, in the next meeting, I would move to the imagery fairly quickly so that there is time to give it the attention needed. I have worked outpatient on a consultant basis and have used imagery without feeling pressed by time, but I have also never been in a situation where I had to shut down trauma imagery midstream. I would assume you would want to provide some time for the closure and leave the door open to come back to it in the next session.

Aslan

I like this particular story because it was unique in several ways. It had a different manifestation of the Divine than I had previously heard, which I thought was interesting and made it memorable. The other feature that was unique was when the client developed the "plan" for intervening they created a plan, but its implementation went much differently than he had created in his mind's eye. The exciting things about it not going the way he had imagined in his own mind is the fact that imagery can truly be an organic in the moment experience that goes in unexpected directions. When doing imagery with people it is important to set aside any preconceived ideas and to focus on the superstructure, but not the moment to moment experience.

This imagery was done with an adult male. He had a long history of self-destructive behaviors including high-risk sexual encounters with strangers, intensive substance abuse, and criminal involvement. He had been in and out of rehab over a dozen times before we met. His history was riddled with high-intensity trauma experiences. He and I used trauma imagery for an experience he had when he was a young child.

His neighbor came to visit his house. The neighbor threatened the young child's life if he left the living room. The man went to the kitchen where the child's mother was at the time and then sexually violated her there in the kitchen. My young client was in the next room the entire time, scared to death and uncertain what to do. He was so ashamed of himself for failing to protect his mother, and they had never talked about the incident, even after thirty years had passed.

I cannot recall the context of the conversation when this emerged; but this young man, whom we will call Aslan, had been working on some feelings of powerless and inadequacy. When asked if there were other times in this life when he had felt that way, he remembered the story involving a neighbor sexually abusing his mom. Aslan had a lot of resentment towards his neighbor, not only for what he did to his mother, but for making him feel powerless, which was a feeling that he had been left with for much of his life, a feeling of not being enough and not being capable. After hearing his story, I asked him, "Do you want to do something a little bit weird?" He consented, and we began the imagery process. He closed his eyes and imagined "a group of people with [his] best interest at heart." Then he asked the group, "Do you love me?" He repeated this process with his Higher Power, imagining it to be a larger-than-life lion with a magnificent, majestic mane, "Do you love me?" He identified two people that wanted to help him with something difficult. Aslan then asked his Higher Power to take him back to the memory, understanding that he had the ability to stop the session at any time and that he would not be reliving the memory to re-experience it but to have the ability to "fix it."

Once the preliminaries were established, Aslan went back to the memory. He took time to create a plan. There was a pretty good period of silence before he was ready. When he was ready, he told me later that he and his dream team had developed a plan to protect his mother. The plan was that he and the dream team were going to rush into the kitchen and protect his mother while the Lion bit off the head of the neighbor.

When Aslan enacted his plan, his younger self took the hands of his two dream team members and the adult Aslan, and they rushed into the kitchen and stood in between the neighbor and Aslan's mother. He and his team wrapped her in a hug and waited for the Lion to eat the head of the neighbor. However, in Aslan's mind, instead of the Lion running in and ripping the neighbor's head off with the fury that Aslan harbored in his resentful, anger-based plan, the Lion calmly walked in, walked right up to the neighbor, and stared him in the eyes. The neighbor flushed red with fear and embarrassment and then walked away with his head hanging and arms slumped in shame. After he had left the house, the Lion went to the dream team that was wrapping the mom up in a hug, and Aslan felt a warm, rich forgiving love wash over his entire system.

Initially Aslan felt disappointed when the man's head was not ripped off his body, but then Aslan felt a deep sense of pity for this neighbor for whom Aslan had hated for most of his life. Aslan gained a sense of liberation and empowerment. He felt the warmth and love of his Higher Power and his dream team. He felt a little part of him was made whole again.

Conclusion

When we access memory, we change memory. This is an important dynamic in therapy because as we get in and manipulate traumatic memory, we are re-writing the memory. We give people the opportunity to gain power over their stories. In place of having the story shape you, you begin to shape the story. This is empowering and client centered. It does not foster dependence on a clinician, but it does provide clients with the skill set to work on their own trauma memories and experiences. After being introduced to the process, I have had clients that report waking up to a trauma dream and instead of waiting for therapy, they lay in their bed and run a meditation similar to the imagery described above. They connect to people that have their best interest at heart and their Higher Power, and then they reshape the story of the dream. They "fix it."

Can you see how this can be empowering as a therapist? In the field, we often joke that our real goal is to work ourselves out of business. Meaning, in a perfect world, no one would need our services. Then we can all go into sales or other market driven jobs (just kidding). Unfortunately, pain and suffering are so prevalent I don't for see a time that we will actually work ourselves out of business, but I would love to know that a client's life has been touched in such a way that they found a new start. I would love to know that they were not dependent on therapy for the rest of their life in a fight for survival but that they have achieved a personal place of strength. I can't throw back every starfish washed up onto shore, but I can make a difference to "this one."

On the other hand, this work is loving. It is powerful. It is healing. It is inspiring. There is a quote I read once that I love: "Effective therapy is an engagement of two people that leaves both changed. If only one changes the therapy has been a failure" (Longo, 2005). This really resonates with me. I know that I am a better person because of these experiences with my clients. As they face their daemons and knit back together their fragmented souls, I am inspired to do the same in my own life.

Trauma Imagery

In the next chapter, we are going to explore generational interconnectedness and the powerful shift that can happen in clients as they look beyond themselves. Like backpacking in the wilderness and becoming incredibly worn and tired, so they are invited to reach out beyond themselves.

Trauma Template Review

- Imagine a group of people that have your best interest at heart. They can be alive or dead, known or unknown, anyone throughout all humanity, but they must have this one common interest… your best interest at heart. Once they are collected in your mind's eye I want you to give me a thumbs up or a grunt or indicate to me somehow that you can see them or sense them or whatever.
- Now I want you to ask that group of people that has your best interest at heart, Do you love me? And feel the response!
- Imagine that from among this group of people that has your best interest at heart steps forward your Higher Power, God, Mother God, Vishnu, Buddha, Allah, Christ, whatever that looks like to you. I want you to connect with that power, with that essence.
- Now I want you to ask the same question, Do you love me? And feel the response!
- Look back over the group of people that has your best interest at heart, and ask for two volunteers, two people that would be willing to help you work through hard emotional work and support you through this process.
- You can tell me who those two people are if you would like, and I will use their names throughout the imagery. If you prefer, you can just hold onto that information. Do you want to share the names?
- Ok, this represents your dream team. There is you, your Higher Power, and [identified volunteers].
- Imagine a vehicle of some sort. It can be a car, boat, plane—whatever you want. Once you establish the vehicle that makes sense to you, I want you to get into the vehicle along with your dream team. Then turn to your Higher Power and ask that being to bring you and your dream team back to that event. *But*, before you go there, I want to emphasize a few things. Because this is in your mind's eye, you have a lot of control over what happens. In your mind, you can put things on pause, you can rewind or fast forward, you can make things small, you can make

things big, you can make things black and white. Your mind is a magical place, so you are not going to relive anything or re-experience the event; you are going to reshape, change, and manipulate the memory of the experience.

- Go ahead and have you're Higher Power take you back to the time of the event. You and the dream team will not travel right into the middle of the situation but just outside the home or place of the event, so you are in the space but not in the event. Let me know when you get there.
- Now I want you to come up with a plan. You and the dream team are going to work together to set this situation right. What happened to you was not your fault. And it is not fair that it happened. You and the dream team are going to come up with a plan to 'fixing it.' Any of the players can be involved in any way that you want. Once you have a plan—take as long as you want—let me know.
- Ok, go and do the plan. Make it happen. Fix it. Take as long as you want. Let me know when you are done.
- Now that you are in this safe place, I just want you to give the little you a big hug. I want you to love that part of yourself. Tell him/her how strong, beautiful, and awesome he/she is. Ask the little you if there is anything he/she want to communicate to you. Take as long as you need. Let me know when you are done.
- Now I want you to give [identified volunteers] a big hug. I want you to feel their arms around you, and I want you to feel their love for you. As you are giving them a hug, I want you to just whisper in their ear anything you would want to tell them, anything you want them to know. Then listen to what they have to say to you. Take as long as you want. Let me know when you're done.
- Now I want you to give a big hug to your Higher Power, and feel the love. Within this embrace I want you to tell them anything you need them to know. Then listen to what your Higher Power has to say to you. Take as long as you want. Let me know when you're done.
- When you are ready, open your eyes.

FAMILY PLAGUE

Ancestor Veneration

It has been documented that almost 1 out of every 200 internet searches is related to genealogy. Virtually every major website that create online searchable genealogical data and allow for users to compile and link personal records with archived records has (records growth at about 20% a year Ancestry.com, MyHeratage, FamilySearch, Geni.com, etc.). There seems to be a global hunger to connect with one's ancestral roots. This is not just a recent development, but cultures throughout history have engaged, to some degree, in ancestral veneration. In other words, there are rituals and rites that are infused into societies throughout the world that help them remember their deceased loved ones. Such practices can be found in China, Japan, Mexico, India, Egypt, Africa, ancient Rome, and many other nations.

Many of these cultures had celebratory rituals in conjunction with the summer solstice. This is a day in June when brighter, longer, spring-summer days begin to transition back to darker, shorter, fall-winter days. In the case of the

Mayan rituals in Mexico, the traditional summer solstice festivities were condemned as pagan by Christian authorities, and many of the rituals related to ancestor worship commuted later in the year to All Saints' Day. In Mexico these festivities have become known as El Dìa de los Muertos, The Day of the Dead.

On El Dìa de los Muertos, we remember our ancestors by placing their photos in a decorated area with some of their favorite foods and trinkets. In return our deceased relatives visit and spend time with us. It is a way of creating a multigenerational connection that adds depths and meaning to life. In remembering our ancestors, we are more likely to feel a sense of purpose and connection in our own lives.

My wife and I have felt this sense of purpose and connection as we recently received our DNA test from Ancestory.com. Ancestry.com's test analyzes a person's DNA and maps the person's general ethnic ancestry. She and I both collected DNA samples by spitting into a little tube and shipping them off to a lab. She was told by friends, in preparing to do this activity, that it was important she prepare herself because there are times when you dig into family history that "family secrets" reveal themselves as not so "secret."

By way of illustration, my wife's friend, who we will call Bae Felled, learned through DNA testing that her father was not actually biological siblings with the rest of his sibling set. He had a different father. Bae has yet to reveal this information to her father because she is unsure if the information would do more damage than good. Nevertheless, the warning was illustrative of the muddy mess that makes up family. Despite Bae Felled's reticence to talk with her father about it, it has been my experience that dealing with reality on its own terms is almost always the best policy. Sooner or later, secrets percolate until they reveal themselves. Nothing is truly hidden.

We have yet to receive the results to our DNA tests, and I am excited to measure my DNA results against my limited understanding of where my people came from. As I've waited, I find myself reflecting more on the relatives I remember that have passed on and what it means to be a Rockwood. But the point is something inside of us shifts when we focus beyond ourselves.

While working at a drug and alcohol facility for adolescents, I developed a line of questioning that would challenge some of the pro-substance attitudes that were so prevalent in that environment. Young people would wax poetic about the benefits of psychedelics and how cultures throughout history had used them to open their minds and connect with the Divine. I would occasionally challenge this thinking with a question about the future and their own hypothetical children: 'Would you be willing to introduce your own children to drugs?' Most of these pro-substance fanatics would frantically backpedal: they advocated drugs, but few wanted to be the instrument that introduced their own children to them.

These types of interactions are tricky because it is important not to be condescending or judgmental in the interaction. Adolescents can pick that up in an instant and the conversation is over. But in the right setting, if done in curiosity (as opposed to judgement) and in a relationship of trust, this can be an awesome segue to looking at additional layers of attitude about drug use. There are times it helps to open their eyes in such a way that they can look at their substance abuse through a new lens.

The point of these stories is that when someone thinks outside of his or her ego-centric self-interest, his or her mind opens to new possibilities. From a purely neuropsychological perspective, when you ask someone a question about an attitude or behavior and he or she responds from his or her own perspective, there is an entire network of neurons that will light up; but if you ask the same question and he or she answers from another's perspective, a completely different neuro net will fire up. This allows someone to access insight, motivation, and strength in a different way than if he or she was to simply analyze the situation from his or her own perspective even though his or her own brain is ultimately the source of the insight in both situations.

The following imagery template helps a client tap into a new way of thinking that ties past and future generations into the motivational framework.

Family Plague Template

I usually use the family plague template with behaviors that have an intergenerational component to them. That also happens to be the areas I have worked in the most throughout my career: sexual and substance abuse. Both of these have a clear intergenerational transmission component.

The mechanics will start out the same as we have discussed. I would have the client get comfortable while lying on the couch or sitting comfortable. Have them close his or her eyes, and then say to them, "Imagine a group of people that have your best interest at heart. They can be alive or dead, known or unknown, anyone throughout all humanity, but they must have this one thing in common: your best interest at heart. When you can see them gathered together or you can sense them in your mind's eye, let me know." Pause. "Now ask them, Do you love me? And feel the response!

Family Plague

"Now imagine your Higher Power, the Universe, Mother God, Vishnu, Buddha, Allah, Christ, whatever that looks like to you. Connect with that being, that entity, that person." Pause. "And ask them the same question: Do you love me? And feel the response!

"As you are in this loving and peaceful place, I want you to imagine a grassy hill. Imagine a hill that is isolated from other hills. There aren't any trees or shrubs or other visual obstructions. This hill must stand all alone in the middle of a vast field that stretches out in all directions for a huge length. Have you ever seen a place like that? Tell me about it."

If the client has a place in mind, using the images and symbols from that memory can add layers of personal connection to the vision. If the client hasn't, you and the client together can co-create an image of the space. Then continue: "I want you to imagine yourself on the top of the hill. Imagine that as you look down, you have a perfect view of the valley to each side of you. The valley is not some small meadow; it is a few football fields long on both sides.

"Now I want you to imagine off to your left in the valley all of your family that came before you. Imagine your parents, aunts and uncles, grandparents, the siblings of your grandparents, your great, great grandparents and their siblings and kids, and just keep going back generation after generation until you have filled up this vast field with your ancestors. Let me know when you can see them in your mind's eye.

"Ok, I know this is going to sound weird, but I want you to imagine a neon bright color. You know, one of those colors that looks like it would glow in the dark. It can be neon pink, orange, blue, yellow, whatever. The only requirement is that is intense and vivid. You got it? What color is it? I want you to imagine that you have a powerful spray paint can of that stuff. This is no ordinary spray can. Let me tell you about the magical properties of this crazy paint.

"You know how you have struggled with drinking since you were just an ankle biter. How you would pilfer drinks from your parent's liquor cabinet. Do you think you were the only kid that has ever done something like that? No, of course not. Do you think it is possible maybe even your parents or one of your aunts or uncles might have done something like that when they were younger?

"Here is the deal. Lots of times these types of problems are not created from nowhere. In fact, there is some evidence that substance abuse is in part a genetic disorder, meaning that addiction is in your chemical makeup. That is why it was harder for you to get drunk than it was for your friends. You thought it was so cool you could 'hold your liquor,' but that just means that you come from a family that has been drinking generation after generation. And not all of that was responsible drinking either.

"I want you to imagine pointing that magical neon paint can in the direction of all your family members. Spray out a mist of the stuff. This is a crazy powerful can, so it is going to spray out a mist that goes from the foot of the hill you're standing on all the way to the people in the very back of the crowd. But this paint is not normal. This paint sticks onto people only if they have struggled with substance abuse. That can be drinking, drugging, or whatever. But if they are like the straight-laced sober type, the paint just blows right passed them. Do you get what I am saying? What will end up happening is anyone that has abused substances will pop out of the crowed covered in neon paint, and the sober types will just look normal.

"Don't worry—the paint isn't toxic, so they will be fine. But I want you to look out over that group, and I want you to try to guess the percentage of people that you see that paint stick to. How many of them have had experiences where maybe they couldn't stop after just a drink or two? How many of them have done something that they were super embarrassed about after they sobered up? How many have gaps in their memory because of their substance use? Worse yet, how many of them died or hurt someone else as a result of their substance abuse? How many had complications while using or accidents in conjunction with using?

"Tell me what percentage of the people that you can see have been touched by these kinds of addictions?" When they answer this question, my clients consistently give a number between 80% and 90%. Ultimately it does not matter exactly what number they give you, but my experience is that it is often quite high.

Once this first phase is established, I have the client look around to the other side of the field. I say, "On the right side of this field is your future kids. It is your nieces and nephews. It is your grand kids, and your grandkid's grandkids. These are the future generations that will come after you. I want you to fill up the football fields on this side of the hill. Go as far as you need so that it is as packed as the left side with all the ancestors that came before you.

"Once you can see the entire group of your descendants, I want you to bust out your magical neon paint can again. You may see where this is going. We know that you said you saw 90% of your ancestors to the left side have been negatively affected and impacted in some way by substance abuse. We also know that unfortunately you have upheld the family tradition and have gotten caught up and lost in that world for a long time. You have been struggling with this stuff for years. Let's just pretend for a minute that this pattern never changes, and down the road you are grown up and you have some kids, your kids have kids, and so forth as you can see out to the right side here.

"I want you to imagine never changing. If you don't do anything about your addiction, how will that impact the lives of all these people that are stretched out on the right side in this valley? Take that crazy magical neon spray can and coat the crowd. Spray out a neon mist over all your kids, grandkids, and great grandkids—all that you can see in the field. Let the mist settle, and because it has the magical properties we already discussed, it will stick only to the people that will struggle and be negatively impacted by substance abuse, kids that may go through some of the things you have experienced or worse.

"Once that neon settles onto the crowd, I want you to look out over these future generations and tell me what percentage of them will struggle with addiction issues if you just stay the same and never chose to change?" The numbers here are typically near the ones for the ancestors on the left. Substance abuse will touch the lives of the vast majority: 80–90%.

"Ok, now that we have looked at what came before you and what could potentially come after you, I want you to think about something a little crazy. I want you to imagine that right now, with no qualms or hesitations, you totally change your life around and magically you become straitlaced and sober for the rest of your life. Think about it like being born again into this alternative life where you are sober and happy and a more caring, selfless, and empowered person or being.

"With that change in mind, with a total transformation of heart, I want you to again look out to the group on the right side. This is your kids and your kids' kids going forward for many, many years. Imagine that they are all magically cleaned up from the neon paint. Look at them like you were looking at them for the first time. I want you to take that magical paint can and do the same exercise. In the event you have totally embraced change so that you are in a different place as you raise and care for your own kids, and they are in a different place as they raise and care for their own kids, I want you to mist the crowed with the neon paint again. Get a good mist over the entire crowd, and as the magical paint settles, it only sticks to the people that will struggle with substance abuse in the future.

"As you look over this crowd, as the paint settles, tell me what percentage of the crowed pops out in neon. If you change, how does that affect the possibility of the future?" At this point, the client will commonly reverse whatever numbers he or she had stated previously. Under the first condition where the client did not change, 90% of the crowed struggled with substance abuse issues; now after changing the variable of him or herself, as the client looks out over the future generations, he or she will report as few as 10% being dowsed in color. Typically—not always since absolutes are *never* true—there is a major shift in the proportion of people the client identifies as struggling with addiction (or whatever issue is being addressed).

Odie Umh

I introduced Odie Umh earlier and shared the perfect storm of trauma that brought him into my residential treatment center as a budding teenager. Unfortunately, he was there until he aged out of the system as an eighteen-year-old. Certainly, this would qualify of as non-traditional upbringing. You may remember that this was a young man whose past was riddled with trauma including neglect and sexual abuse. He is one of the many clients that have worked through the family plague imagery. His story sticks out because of the monumental impact that it had on his personal emotional growth, and this imagery refocused him in a way that he went from struggling with total emotional dysregulation and chaos to a more focused and motivated disposition.

At the time I introduced Odie to family plague imagery, he was really struggling on the unit, and he was having a hard time connecting with his peers. He was angry all the time, and he would act out in such a way that would leave the entire system in disarray. At times he was violent towards others; or he could be sexual with or around peers. Staff were passive-aggressively trying to get him kicked out of the facility by complaining to management about the laundry list of problems he was creating. The staff felt that he took so much attention that it set them up to have problems with the other kids. They worried that spending so much time supervising Odie individually, that it was difficult to manage the larger group. They worried that Odie's bad example would inspire others to engage in disruptive behaviors.

Once when Odie and I were talking in session, about his experience as a sexual abuse victim and perpetrator, family plague imagery came to my mind, so I asked him to close his eyes. He lay down on the couch and made himself comfortable. We simultaneously took deep breaths together. We would often do some activity to become synchronized because of the early attachment disruptions for this young man. We would breath in synch, sing together, do "paced" walks, and even pull faces and mirror each other—anything to fire up mirror neurons and stimulate the attachment centers of the brain.

Family Plague

After doing some relaxation breathing, I then asked him, "Imagine a group of people that have your best interest at heart. They can be alive or dead, known or unknown, anyone throughout all humanity but they must have this one common theme: your best interest at heart. Once you see them in your mind's eye or you can sense their presence. I want you to let me know. Ask that group of people that has your best interest at heart, Do you love me? And feel the response."

As I described earlier, you would think with Odie's past and unstable life that he would have a really hard time connecting with this type of instruction. Despite all this, Odie Umh did not. Whenever we did any kind of guided imagery, he could always find that group, even though at times it only consisted of staff and therapists and people that surrounded him every day in the facility. He would often include in his imageries one of the proctor families he had lived with. The father in the family was a Christian youth minister and had really fostered a strong bond with Odie. Despite living in another state, the father visited Odie several times over the years he was in the group home.

Once we got through the first step, I asked him, "Now I want you to imagine that from among this group of people that have your best interest at heart steps forward Christ. Connect with him. Look him in the eyes, and ask him this question: Do you love me? And feel the response." Because of Odie's strong attachment to Christianity and knowing he used Christ to represent the Higher Power, I would use that specific iconography to match Odie's interest and the narrative he created for himself. Other students have used Mother Earth, the Universe, their Eternal Self or a host of other Deities. I am not invested in shaping their conceptualization of the Divine, but I will use whatever their articulated Divinity might be. Not only is such an approach client centered, it seems to amplify the experience if you use their own language in the imagery.

Once we were connected on these levels, I asked, "Have you ever been atop a big hill that allowed you to see a huge space that stretched out for a long, long way? Like several football fields stretched out in all directions (or at least two)?" Odie could identify a cool hill he had been to while on an activity at another facility, so I told him to stand on top of that hill in his mind.

Once he gave me the signal, I told him, "Look off to the right and imagine all of your family that came before you. Your parents, aunts and uncles, grandparents, their siblings, going back generation after generation until they filled up that space." When that was in his mind's eye, he then picked a bright, vibrant color that would pop and be easy for him to see. He wanted to use bright pink. I told him, "Imagine the 'magic spray can' and spray out over that group of people, but remember that the pink will only stick to people that had sexually harmed others or that had been sexually harmed themselves."

I asked him what percentage of the group had been affected by the neon pink, and he replied that it was about 90%. I then directed, "I want you to look out to the vast space on the left. Imagine your kids and grandkids and their partners and the generations after that. Go on and on until they fill up that side of the valley. Imagine that you never changed and just continued the path you have been on before getting into treatment, where you hurt the people around you by acting out your trauma on others and perpetuating the cycle of pain and abuse. Imagine once again your magic paint can and paint this group of future generations. Your children and grandchildren down the generations. Let the paint settle and then tell me what percentage was impacted by the abuse or by abusing others." Odie reported 100%.

It is rare someone takes an all or nothing approach like that, but the numbers don't really matter, and so I just continued the imagery session. I then told him, "Imagine that instead of the last scenario we described where you continued to hurt others, imagine yourself magically changed. You are different. You can stop the cycle that had created so much damage and torn your family apart. Imagine that you are the change agent in your family system. Now grab that bright pink magical paint can and spray out over your kids, grand kids, and down the line. I want you to imagine that the paint only sticks to those who are sexually abused or who abuse others. As you look out over this group of future generations, how many show up with the hot pink paint on them?"

With tears in his eyes, he says, "Maybe 10%."

"Isn't it crazy that it went from everyone to just a small group?" His emotional response to the imagery made me curious, and I prodded him a little further: "As you are there on the hill, what do you see?"

I will never forget his response. He still had his eyes closed with moistened cheeks, and he exclaimed in an empowered voice, "I see me dressed all in white. I have a pillar of light around me that ascends to the heavens, and I am an angel of God. No, not an angel, a *warrior*! I am God's warrior for making change in my family. I can do this!"

Chills ran down my spine to hear him talk like that. I know that he meant it. There was a dramatic shift in his overall attitude and presentation from that day on. That is not to say he was "healed" or that life went perfectly, but it was a monumental shift that began to redefine how he saw himself.

Conclusion

What I am describing here is not a psychotic break where Odie Umh is out of touch with reality. Family plague imagery is simply a re-storying of one's experience. It is a new way of looking at the past and the future. Odie's decision to take on the challenge of being a "warrior" fundamentally changed his approach to life.

Odie Umh had been in therapy virtually his entire life. He had tried to learn coping skills, and he tried to be aware of thinking errors and reframe his negative thoughts. He was familiar with cycle work and patterns that emerged in his interactions with others that got in the way of his success. He could prattle along with therapeutic jargon all day long and at times talk a good game. But there had never been that fundamental shift in his heart.

I have heard it said that one of the hardest journeys we can ever make is the fourteen-inch journey from our head to our heart (Jones, 2010). Odie Umh knew what he needed to do. He could list off coping skills with the best of them. He just did not live what he preached. There was cognitive dissonance between what he knew and the way he acted.

That day he embraced a new story and in so doing found something he was willing to fight for. The shame that comes from feeling broken and unlovable was framed not as a personal flaw but as a generational curse that was passed down from father and mother to son and daughter. Odie lacked the self-love and self-confidence to fight for his own healing, but he was not going to let his children and grandchildren suffer because of him. He was to become the agent of change—an agent for his posterity and a teammate for himself.

When we look beyond the ego, beyond the self, there is a strength and a resolve that can be drawn from that has the potential to make a difference. For many of us professionals who help victims of sexual abuse there is a theme that quickly emerges. I cannot tell you how many times I've been working with a victim who has for years suffered in silence only to break the silence when they learn that there is another victim. A young man may be sexually abused by his father for years only to learn that the father has moved on to a younger sibling, and so the young man breaks the silence.

Family plague imagery in broad application has therapeutic power. This is an option that has power to expand a client's world view and stoke the fire of resolve. The brain literally draws from fundamentally different resources (neural nets) when the focus changes from oneself to others. And there is value drawing from any source that can assist and support healing in our clients.

Family Plague

Family Plague Template

- Imagine a group of people that have your best interest at heart. They can be alive or dead, known or unknown, anyone throughout all humanity, but they must have this one thing in common, your best interest at heart. When you can see them gathered together or you can sense them in your mind's eye, let me know.

- Now ask them, Do you love me? And feel the response!

- Now imagine your Higher Power, the Universe, Mother God, Vishnu, Buddha, Allah, Christ, whatever that looks like to you. Connect with that being, that entity, that divinity.

- And ask them the same question: Do you love me? And feel the response!

- As you are in this loving and peaceful place, I want you to imagine a grassy hill. Imagine a hill that is isolated from other hills. There aren't any trees or shrubs or other visual obstructions. This hill must stand all alone in the middle of a vast field that stretches out in all directions for a huge length. Have you ever seen a place like that? Tell me about it.

- I want you to imagine yourself on the top of the hill. Imagine that as you look down, you have a perfect view of the valley to each side of you. The valley is not some small meadow; it is a few football fields long on both sides.

- Now I want you to imagine off to your left in the valley all of your family that came before you. Imagine your parents, cousins, aunts and uncles, grandparents, the siblings of your grandparents, your great, great grandparents and their siblings and kids, and just keep going back generation after generation until you have filled up this vast field with your ancestors. Let me know when you can see them in your mind's eye.

- Ok, I know this is going to sound weird, but I want you to imagine a neon bright color. You know, one of those colors that looks like it would glow in the dark. It can be neon pink, orange, blue, yellow, whatever. The only requirement is that is intense and vivid. You got it? What color is it? I want you to imagine that you have a powerful spray paint can of that stuff. This is no ordinary spray can. Let me tell you about the magical properties of this crazy paint.

- You know how you have struggled with [addiction, drinking, eating disorder, violence, etc.] Do you think you were the only kid that has ever done something like that? No, of course not. Do you think it is possible maybe even your parents or one of your aunts or uncles might have done something like that when they were younger?

- I want you to imagine pointing that magical neon paint can in the direction of all your family members. Spray out a mist of the stuff. This is a crazy powerful can, so it is going to spray out a mist that goes from the foot of the hill you're standing on all the way to the people in the very back of the crowd. But this paint is not normal. This paint sticks onto people only if they have struggled with [focus problem]. What will end up happening is anyone that has [focus problem] will pop out of the crowed covered in neon paint, and the others will just look normal.

- Don't worry—the paint isn't toxic, so they will be fine. But I want you to look out over that group, and I want you to try to guess the percentage of people that you see that paint stick to.

- Tell me what percentage of the people that you can see have been touched by these kinds of addictions?

- On the right side of this field is your future kids. It is your nieces and nephews. It is your grand kids, and your grandkid's grandkids. These are the future generations that will come after you. I want you to fill up the football fields on this side of the hill. Go as far as you need so that it is as packed as the left side with all the ancestors that came before you.

- Once you can see the entire group of your descendants, I want you to bust out your magical neon paint can again. You may see where this is going. We know that you said you saw [percentage they gave earlier] of your ancestors to the left side have been negatively affected and impacted in some way by [focus problem]. We also know that unfortunately you have upheld the family tradition and have gotten caught up and lost in that world for a long time. You have been struggling with this stuff for years. Let's just pretend for a minute that this pattern never changes, and down the road you are grown up and you have some kids, your kids have kids, and so forth as you can see out to the right side here.

- I want you to imagine never changing. If you don't do anything about your [focus problem], how will that impact the lives of all these people that are stretched out on the right side in this valley? Take that crazy magical neon spray can and coat the crowd. Spray out a neon mist over all your kids, grandkids, and great grandkids—all that you can see in the field. Let the mist settle, and because it has the magical properties we already discussed, it will stick only to the people that will struggle and be negatively impacted by [focus problem], kids that may go through some of the things you have experienced or worse.

- Once that neon settles onto the crowd, I want you to look out over these future generations and tell me what percentage of them will struggle with [focus problem] if you just stay the same and never chose to change?

- Ok, now that we have looked at what came before you and what could potentially come after you, I want you to think about something a little crazy. I want you to imagine that right now, with no qualms or hesitations, you totally change your life around and magically you become [opposite focus problem] for the rest of your life. Think about it like being born again into this alternative life where you are happy and a more caring, selfless, and empowered person or being.

- With that change in mind, with a total transformation of heart, I want you to again look out to the group on the right side. This is your kids and your kids' kids going forward for many, many years. Imagine that they are all magically cleaned up from the neon paint. Look at them like you were looking at them for the first time. I want you to take that magical paint can and do the same exercise. In the event you have totally embraced change so that you are in a different place as you raise and care for your own kids, and they are in a different place as they raise and care for their own kids, I want you to mist the crowed with the neon paint again. Get a good mist over the entire crowd, and as the magical paint settles, it only sticks to the people that will struggle with [focus problem] in the future.

- As you look over this crowd, as the dust settles, tell me what percentage of the crowed pops out in neon. If you change, how does that affect the possibility of the future?
- When you are ready, open your eyes, and come back to this place.

WEAK LINK/EGO-STATE

Squad

Imagine for a moment that you are serving in the armed services. You are assigned to a squad of nine other soldiers. Your assignment is to be the forward eyes for your company as you slowly work your way deeper into enemy territory. One of the great challenges is that it is difficult to know who are hostile and who are innocent civilians caught in the chaos of the war.

After all the intensive training that you have engaged in over the last year, you feel emotionally closer to your squad than to anyone else on the planet. It surprises you at times how they seem to be more attuned to your moods and needs than anyone you have ever met. Calling them family would not stray from the core feeling you have working with them. You know that they have your back, and you have theirs.

One day while on patrols, an improvised explosive device is triggered, and there is a huge explosion. Your ears are ringing and all noise seems to be muted. You quickly assess the situation and realize that there are not life-threatening injuries in the squad, a few dings and scratches but nothing life threatening. One of your mates has a dent in his helmet where he was struck by a blunt object, and you count your lucky stars for the high-quality safety equipment. There is no doubt it saved a life today.

A few days go by, and your squad is once again on patrol. While combing the area, you notice that your mate seems to have a distant look in his eyes, and he is muttering to himself. You try to focus enough to pick up on what he is saying, but it seems like a nonsensical stream of incoherent and unconnected words. Something is clearly wrong. You feel an internal struggle as to what should happen next. Every member of the squad is vital for the success of each mission—and for the safety of each member.

Later that night, you express some of your thoughts and concerns to other members of the squad. They had also picked up on the personality shift and abnormal behavior of your mate. That confirms it is not something you are imagining, but something is clearly wrong with your mate. Perhaps the blast and the damaged helmet had been more than just a close call. There is a possibility something about that blast that did something to your mate, it altered him.

The catch-22 is that all of you love and trust your mate fully when his wits are about him, but if you were to forward the change in his behavior to the platoon commander, your mate is likely headed back to the forward operational base. Your strong emotional connection to your mate triggers hesitation to have him shipped out of your squad. But on the other hand, if he is not at the top of his game, not only is his life in danger, but everyone in the squad may be placed at risk.

As a group, you and the rest of the squad invite your mate into the discussion about your concerns and observations. He states that he feels fine and feels like people are blowing things out of proportion. He lacks an awareness of his incoherent chatter and denies that any such rambling transpired. In this exchange, your mate starts to get emotionally escalated defending himself. He seems to realize that the concern is that maybe he is not in his right mind. He is insulted, hurt, and angry by the accusation.

It becomes clear that his denial and lack of awareness are a sign that things are unlikely to change. After some deliberation, it is decided that making a report up the chain of command is the only way to protect your mate from himself while at the same time protecting the squad. The issue is simply that the squad is only as strong as the weakest member. Therefore, it is important to help the weakest link in the chain to perform at its very best; sometimes that requires intervention and outside help.

Fudgesicle 500

The wilderness trips with the boys and Dr. Gary Weaver included a fifty-mile hike through a series of slot canyons. Throughout the backpacking trip, we had several groups that were integrated into the flow of the experience. These group sessions were designed using the unique features of the environment and wilderness space around us.

Many of the activities had in mind the idea of building the group up as a cohesive unit. There were certainly some activities that were more individual challenges, but the vast majority were more group oriented. The boys would be invited to take on challenges that would inevitably require a variety of skills and teamwork in order to be completed.

The very last group of the trip was one of my favorites. Gary called it the Fudgesicle 500. I asked him where he came up with the name, and he told me that he wanted it to sound like a race out of Daytona. There was no specific meaning to the 500, but it just sounded cool and important. The last day (Saturday) of this six-day adventure, we had a final challenge: the Fudgesicle 500. The goal was to travel the last three miles of the hike to the vans in one hour. If successful, they will get an ice cream treat at the first convenience station we pass on the way home. But, this is not an individual challenge; this is a group challenge: even if some arrive at the vans before the hour is up, if the slowest member of the group arrives even one minute late, then no one gets the reward.

In every group that has ever gone out with us, there are both strong hikers and not so strong hikers. Many of you will recognize that traveling three miles in one hour is not exactly breaking speed barriers, but to put the Fudgesicle 500 in perspective, when traveling with a group of youth in the wilderness, backpacks loaded down with gear, and a winding up path with rises and falls, the experience is quite different from running around a track or a neighborhood.

Between where the boys start and the vans, the boys would cross the river about seven times. "River" may be an overstatement since it is only about knee deep, but each crossing included dropping down one bank and scrambling up the other side. There are also sections of the desert path that are very fine desert sand; when hiking on such a trail, it feels like for every step you lose a half a step sliding and sinking in the soft sand—and you need to periodically empty your shoes of this sand so you don't get massive blisters.

I would give the boys a little pep talk as we introduced the activity. I would ask them if there was an "I" in the word team. When they would say, "No," and I would then present the argument that there is absolutely an I in the word team. The "I" is my *individual effort*. The "I" is my commitment to the group to ensure its success. Without the "I" in team, I become the weak link. In addition, I would reinforce the idea that I had encouraged them to think about throughout our trip that the leaders are not always at the front of the line. The leaders are the ones that are helpers to those that may have strengths in areas other than wilderness hiking.

I love using chants building and pumping up the boys. Chants can be exhilarating and releases endorphins, and they can have a bonding component when done in unison. Acting in unison fires up our mirror neurons and fosters attachment, which is a constant focus in all my clinical work.

The specific chant I would do with the boys came from an amazing experience I had with an executive training through Discover Leadership Training out of Texas. We would have the boys all huddle up so their arms were draped across one another's shoulders. I would lead the chant and have them echo what I said. We would run through it three times with a crescendo throughout the chant. We would start loud and end at ear-splitting decibels.

The chant looked like this. I would shout, "I am strong!" They would echo this back as a group. If someone was not participating, I would point it out, ask for their support, and repeat the first stage. This was always at the end of our wilderness experience after the boys had already developed a strong group cohesion and team investment, so it was not often that they needed additional coaxing. Then I would continue: "I am powerful!" The group would echo this back. Then I would emphasize, "I am personally responsible!"

We would cycle through these three statements three times: "I am strong! I am powerful! I am personally responsible!" By the end of the third time, there is this total euphoria and overwhelming excitement. As soon as this was done, before anyone could say anything, I would shout, "LET'S

GO! GO, GO, GO!" and then take off running into the first river crossing. Like a swarm, the boys follow with high intensity and commitment.

Now, three miles is a long way. Inevitably during the journey, people would start to lose momentum and stop. The moment someone would stop, everyone stops and encourages and supports that person. I have done this activity sixteen times with different groups, and every time there comes a moment when we have to redistribute the workload. Someone that is really struggling will find relief by giving his backpack to a peer. That peer is now double packing, and the boy without a pack is told that without that weight, he is responsible for keeping up. There are times that we would take long loops of webbing and link a strong hiker with someone that is struggling. There are times that a young man would just have a buddy put a little pressure on his backpack to keep forward momentum.

The exact nature of the help did not matter as long as everyone was mutually supportive and positive. Throughout the wilderness experience, we had emphasized that you never criticize or complain about a peer's performance because nothing is more de-motivating than such negative feedback. So by this final activity, the boys have perfected the art of encouragement without condescension or sarcasm. I will also point out that there have been times when the person struggling the most during the Fudgesicle 500 was not one of the boys but one of our staff. They are included in the challenge, and they need to be successful just as much as the boys, so when needed we have made all of the same accommodations. I have never seen the boys fail the Fudgsicle 500, regardless of the strength of the hikers and the amount of struggle used to make it happen.

One interesting side note is that every once and a while, we have had the strongest hikers convince themselves the best thing they can do is run all the way to the vehicles, drop their packs, and then return to the group and help once they have unburdened themselves. If this is the strategy the group chooses, and the runners have staff to accompany them, this has been allowed. It is interesting that in all of the groups where they accomplished the task in the quickest amount of time, the group stuck together and helped throughout the process. Anytime that strong hikers ran a head and returned to help once they could take off their own bag, the group was skirting into the finish just prior to the hour deadline. There is something more powerful and motivating about doing it together, than to have a knight in shining armor trying to save the group single handedly.

Weal Link Template

In both scenarios I just described, the issues dealt with group dynamics. All the principles of group dynamics can be applied to an individual in ego-state therapy. For those of you familiar with ego-state therapy, the bridge to where we are headed has probably already been made. If this is an unfamiliar term, let me describe a little bit about the purpose and the utility of this type of intervention.

The reality is there are many approaches to ego-state therapy, and I will describe predominantly two versions. As I have emphasized repeatedly throughout this text, guided imagery provides a very loose and flexible template. If you have other versions of this style of intervention, just use the same principles and insert your preferred method. Do not feel pigeonholed into the versions I chose to focus on here.

The basic principle of all ego-state approaches is to subdivide different parts of self. This can be time periods, ages, roles (father/mother, son/daughter, employer/employee, hobbyist, academic, addict, etc.), or emotional parts (anger, happiness, courage, fear, passion, shame, etc.). You can add any other type of division you or your client wants. Sometimes in therapy with kids that have sexually abused others, we separate out their abuser self from themselves.

I like to think of ego-state therapy as group therapy with these different aspects of self. Typically when I am setting this up, I don't really describe what is going to happen. I just tell the client, "Do you want to try something weird?"

Then I ask the client to close his or her eyes, take a few cleansing breaths, and "Imagine a group of people that have your best interest at heart. They can be alive or dead, known or unknown, anyone throughout all humanity but they must have this one common thread: your best interest at heart. Once this group has gathered in your mind's eye, I want you to let me know. You can say 'got it,' give me a thumbs up, whatever; just let me know when you can see them or sense them in your mind's eye."

Once the client indicates, I say, "Now I want you to ask them this question, Do you love me? And feel the response!" After letting the client sense and feel that for a time, I say, "Now I want you to imagine that from among this group of people that has your best interest at heart, steps forward your Higher Power. Mother God, Buddha, Allah, Vishnu, or whatever that looks like to you. I want you to connect with that entity, that power. Look them in the eyes and ask them this question, Do you love me? And feel the response!"

I let the client soak in that feeling for a minute. With the foundations laid, I say, "We are going to do something a bit weird. Because this is in our mind's eye, it is a magical place where virtually anything is possible. What we are going to do is a little bit of group therapy. But this is not a group therapy session you have ever experienced before. We are going to do therapy with the various aspects of yourself."

At this point, I articulate the type of group the client will form. I set the stage with this one a bit more like traditional imagery work by imposing a setting and image rather than drawing it out from the client. That is my way of doing this specific style of imagery, but a client could just as well create his or her own group therapy space filled with personal healing iconography. For this example, I'll use the five core aspects of self of the client: spiritual, emotional, intellectual, physical, and social. In this case, I would have the client imagine a small group therapy room: blank white walls with five comfortable, padded folding chairs forming a circle.

"Imagine entering the room with all five aspects of yourself, and each aspect finds a seat. Pay attention to where they sit and how they are situated in conjunction with one another. Once everyone is settled in, we are going to have an open format. The issue being discussed is the current situation related to your identified problem (addiction, eating disorder, marital problems, depression, etc.). I want you to pay attention to how all five parts of your core selves look at and analyze the problem. What does each of them view as the causes and maintenance factor to the problem."

Once the stage is set, I simply tell them, "I want you to just watch and pay attention to how the therapy session develops and unfolds. Look for any insights about the problem that you may have missed previously. Take as long as you need. We are not in a hurry; just let it play out and let me know when you are done."

I then wait for a signal that they have completed the discussion, verbal or non-verbal that was set up in advance like a thumbs up or saying ok. If very little time has transpired when the client gives the all done sign, I introduce new topics and questions for the group to explore. If very little time has transpired when the client gives the all done sign, I try to encourage more interaction. Much like in live group therapy, Socratic questions and thought-provoking topics usually draw out longer sessions—even though not being privy to the content of the session can be tricky. In the event that there has been a good silent gap and I feel like the client has really taken time to explore whatever is going on, I move more quickly to concluding the group.

In regular, live group therapy, at the time for the group to close, I commonly summarize, highlight, and reinforce primary points that have been discussed. Sometimes I ask the clients to share their take-home thoughts from the session and what they feel like they can incorporate into their experience that week. When I have the clients summarize, it is not uncommon that I will go around the group and let each group member give their personal insights. I prefer this to just opening it up to a few clients to share their thoughts as such usually results in the same few group members providing the summary each time. The downside to having everyone share is basic group think comes into play and they all start repeating other themes that have been mentioned previously. One technique for breaking up that conformity is to say that they each person needs to share something different, don't go in a circle, and then the people that go last have the added challenge of thinking of unique concepts.

In the ego group, I will do the same thing by instructing the client to "summarize to yourself what you have learned from each of the ego states and identify any take home points that you want to focus on this week." After the group closes, I then say, "Imagine connecting with each aspect of your ego. Give each of them a hug, and whispering in their ears a message that starts with the phrase, 'Something I appreciate about your participation in group today was. . . .'" I have them go to each of the ego states—in this example case, all five of the participants: spiritual, emotional, intellectual, physical, and social. "Now embrace all parts of yourself in a group hug. Then, when you're ready, you can open your eyes and come back into this space."

I will then ask the client if he or she wants to talk about the experience. Sometimes clients do and sometimes they don't. Processing the experience with my clients is not the purpose of ego-state therapy. The internal experience is the important part. Remember, one of the goals in this style of therapy is to get out of the way so clients can heal. It is not about us; it is about them.

Champ

The following story is about a young man that was raised for the first eleven years of his life by his grandmother. We will call him Champ. His mom was a drug addict and would come and go from the home, but she was never the real caregiver. He describes his grandmother as worn out and disengaged. She had raised her kids whom had all become drug addicts. A few of them had kids and now she was "stuck" with raising a bunch of grandkids. Three of Champ's cousins who were about seven to ten years older than him also lived in the home. He was the baby of the group.

Unfortunately, Champ was the whipping boy for the older boys. He was unsure if his grandmother knew the extent of the abusive behavior, but if she was aware, she didn't care enough to help him. This created in him an intense sense of shame and a core belief that he was unlovable.

Eventually he was removed from the home and placed into foster care where he was adopted by the family that took him in. Following the common story of many of my clients, Champ as a teenager started to sexually abuse the younger siblings in the home. As a result, he was sent into residential treatment.

I worked with him while he was in treatment. During one session, he talked about an overall sense that anyone he cares about will either hurt him or leave him. In the course of the conversation, the idea that this young man had a wounded child within him came to my mind, and I felt that ego-state guided imagery could help him. The following is a recreation of the guided imagery, to the best of my recollection.

"Champ, would you be ok if we did something a bit weird?" He assented, and I instructed him to close his eyes and take a few deep cleansing breaths following my lead. Then I said, "Imagine a group of people that have your best interest at heart. They can be alive or dead, known or unknown, anyone throughout all humanity, but they must have your best interest at heart. Let me know when you can see them or sense them.

"Now ask this group of people, Do you love me? And feel the response!" Pause. "Now I want you to imagine that from among this group of people that have your best interest at heart steps forward you're Higher Power. Mother God, Christ, Allah, the Universe, whatever that looks like to you. Connect with this being, this essence, this power; ask the same question: Do you love me? And feel the response!" Pause.

"I want you to imagine a small group therapy room. The room is comfortable and quaint. There are a smattering of about sixteen comfortable, padded folding chairs arranged in a circle. These chairs each have a different *you* sitting in them. There is the one-year-old you, the two-year-old you, the three-year-old you, all the way up to your current self, the sixteen-year-old you. When you can see that in your mind's eye, let me know.

"Next, I want you to imagine that each one of your selves links hands so they are holding the hand to the person to the left and right of them forming a giant circle. Next, I know this is a bit weird, but I want you to imagine that in your sixteen-year-old self a light appears in your chest. Initially I want you to imagine this light as being quite bright. Can you see it?

"Slowly transfer that light down your arm and into the arm of the person next to you. I don't care if it flows to the left or the right; it may go from your sixteen-year-old self to your fifteen-year-old self, or from your sixteen-year-old self to your one-year-old self. Whatever way it flows is fine. I just want you to imagine passing the light so that it travels from one individual to the next.

"Here is the crazy part. As this light passes from one individual to the next, the light will get brighter or dimmer according to the strength or weakness of that particular part of yourself. Let that light flow around the group and pay attention to where it is the dimmest and where it is the brightest. Pass the light around two or three times until you have a real clear idea of what ages experienced the greatest weakness—your weakest links—and what ages experienced the greatest strength—your strongest links.

"Once that passes around a few times and you have a clear sense of the areas of strength and the areas of weakness, let me know. Take as much time as you need. We are not in a hurry. Let me know when you're done." Pause.

Once he was ready, I told him, "I wanted you to take a moment to have those parts of yourself that were the brightest and strongest to nurture and take care of those parts of you that were the dimmest and weakest. That can look however you'd like. Take as much time as you want. Let me know when you are done." Pause.

"Now that you were able to take care of the weakest links, is there any other periods of time that could use some love and nurturing? Take time to engage in the needed self-care for these other parts of yourself. Let me know when you're done." Pause.

"Now that you are done with that, I want your current self, your sixteen-year-old self, to go around the group and tell each one of the ages of your life the thing that you appreciate most about them, and I want you to listen to what they say are the things they most appreciate about you. Take as much time as you need. Let me know when you're done." Pause.

Once Champ has completed this stage, I said, "Imagine a big group hug with the entire crew from the youngest to the oldest. And when you're ready, open your eyes and come on back into this space."

In debriefing the session, Champ indicated he wanted to share a bit about his experience. He said, "I sent the light around, and the brightest moment were my six-year-old self, and the dimmest was just last year when I was fifteen years old." I remember being a bit confused by the identified periods; honestly, I thought that the brightest periods would have been the years of the adoption and the safe home and the hardest periods would be some of the younger years when his mother was not showing up for him, his grandmother was indifferent, and his older siblings (cousins) were virtually torturing him with their emotional and physical brutality.

Champ explained that his young six-year-old self was strong enough to handle the pain and suffering. He felt that he had been protected on some levels by God during those years, and Champ remembers moments he described as being reinforced by his guardian angels. Alternatively, the fifteen-year-old Champ had lost everything through a series of bad choices, by violating the trust of his adopted family, and sexually hurting one of the people he felt the closest to in all the world. It was the fifteen-year-old self that needed to be nurtured, loved, and reinforced, and that reinforcement came from a young self that had a clear vision of his standing and relationship with God and was given the strength to endure serious hardships. This young man shared this story with tears in his eyes, and he articulated how he had forgotten that earlier time in his life until the light triggered the memory of what he had experienced. He indicated after working through things with other stages of his life he could feel the overall brightness of the room enhanced. He felt loved and lovable for the first time in a decade.

Conclusion

Champ's story shows the importance of not having a specific agenda or vision of what is "supposed" to happen. Imagery work at its best is unpredictable and a client-centered intervention. As a therapist, helper, healer, you set the stage and then get out of the way.

If I am serving in a military squadron where my life depends on my mates, and my mates' lives depend on me, I am going to strive for the overall wellbeing of the group. I am going to intervene when something is off. I am not going to ignore the problem or cross my fingers and hope that everything works out.

When I am participating in the Fudgesicle 500 the stakes are clearly not as important as in the squadron. But I learned quickly that sometimes I need help and sometimes I am the helper. The greatest leadership does not come from being in front but working side by side with those that need help the most.

In ego-state therapy, we are looking to build love and cohesion for every part of us, not just for the strong parts or the moments of accomplishment. When I work with people struggling with addiction, they characterize recovery as a fight to kill the addict within. But the addict is part of them. The addict cannot die without a part of them dying as well. The goal is to integrate what was once compartmentalized.

Brene Brown is a researcher in the area of shame who has gifted the world with her personal experience diving into the dark recesses of people's most uncomfortable and hidden secrets. One of the byproducts of her work was the acknowledgement that only when we are completely known, only when all of our faults and imperfections are visible and expressed, only when we have truly been vulnerable, can we feel truly loved, attached, and whole (Brown, 2010). There is something about being known in all our imperfection and yet loved. Not despite such imperfections, but because of them. In that space, there are deep aquafers of healing that can fill our voids and cleanse our souls. There are diamonds to discover and hang onto.

Week Link Template

- Imagine a group of people that have your best interest at heart. They can be alive or dead, known or unknown, anyone throughout all humanity but they must have this one common thread: your best interest at heart. Once this group has gathered in your mind's eye, I want you to let me know. You can say 'got it,' give me a thumbs up, whatever; just let me know when you can see them or sense them in your mind's eye." Now I want you to ask them this question, Do you love me? And feel the response!

- Now I want you to imagine that from among this group of people that has your best interest at heart, steps forward your Higher Power. Mother God, Buddha, Allah, Vishnu, or whatever that looks like to you. I want you to connect with that entity, that power. Look them in the eyes and ask them this question, Do you love me? And feel the response!

- We are going to do something a bit weird. Because this is in our mind's eye, it is a magical place where virtually anything is possible. What we are going to do is a little bit of group therapy. But this is not a group therapy session you have ever experienced before. We are going to do therapy with the various aspects of yourself: spiritual, emotional, intellectual, physical, and social.

- Imagine entering the room with all five aspects of yourself, and each aspect finds a seat. Pay attention to where they sit and how they are situated in conjunction with one another. Once everyone is settled in, we are going to have an open format. The issue being discussed is the current situation related to your identified problem [addiction, eating disorder, marital problems, depression, etc.]. I want you to pay attention to how all five parts of your core selves look at and analyze the problem. What does each of them view as the causes and maintenance factor to the problem.

- I want you to just watch and pay attention to how the therapy session develops and unfolds. Look for any insights about the problem that you may have missed previously. Take as long as you need. We are not in a hurry; just let it play out and let me know when you are done.
- summarize to yourself what you have learned from each of the ego states and identify any take home points that you want to focus on this week.
- Imagine connecting with each aspect of your ego. Give each of them a hug, and whispering in their ears a message that starts with the phrase, 'Something I appreciate about your participation in group today was. . . .'
- Now embrace all parts of yourself in a group hug. Then, when you're ready, you can open your eyes and come back into this space.

ETERNAL SELF

Ugly Duckling

In the mid-1900s, there was a Danish author named Hans Christian Anderson. He wrote several short stories that became quite popular, and later in his life, someone asked if he had any plans to write an autobiography. He responded that he had already written it when he wrote the tale of *The Ugly Duckling*. Hans had grown up tall and gawky. He had a passion for theater, and this did not settle well with his peers who entertained themselves at his expense. It is rumored that as an adult, he learned that he may have been the illegitimate child of royalty. With that as the backdrop, it is interesting to look at the basic narrative flow of *The Ugly Duckling* (Anderson, 2010).

One day a group of ducklings broke free of their eggs. All looked cute and fluffy as new chicks do, but one was grey and misshapen. It looked different than the other ducklings, and the noise that it made was obnoxious and irritating to the other hatchlings. The little grey duck was an embarrassment to the family; he was taunted by its siblings and the ducks in neighboring ponds. Not wanting to be an embarrassment to his family or subjected to the abuse of others in the pond, he ran away. After running through muddy fields and getting covered in grime and muck, he found another pond and another family of ducks who quickly rejected him, and he was forced to continue on his way.

The ugly duckling made another escape, not wanting to be subjected to the abuse of others, and eventually found himself with a family of geese. The geese, like everyone else, made fun of the hatchling's ugliness, but they allowed him to join their family. There he was fairly well-treated and contented for a time. Unfortunately, a hunter and his dog came upon the goose family. The dog recognizing the duckling was not a goose, insulted him, and then captured his adoptive family. The duckling was again left on his own.

Disheveled and too tired to fly, the duckling took shelter near a human home. When he was discovered the next morning, the family took him in hoping to benefit from a duck that could lay eggs for them to eat. When the duckling never produced eggs and became larger and more unmanageable, the farmer family was forced to put him out yet again.

After surviving a cold winter, the duckling found a pond with a group of swans that were magnificent and beautiful. Despite the duckling's longing to be with these birds, he held back knowing that he would again be rejected for his ugliness. Just then, one of the swans flew over to him and complimented his beautiful white plumage. This was the first time the ugly duckling had ever been complimented, and it was disorienting and confusing to him. He approached the water's edge and peered at his reflection only to find a beautiful swan staring back at him.

He was not ugly at all; he was magnificent, and he just had yet to discover it.

It is no wonder that this story has stood the test of time. It is something that many of us can relate too. We all carry negative beliefs about ourselves, often imposed upon us by others; ideally one day we discover that we are more than we had ever imagined or had been told we were. Then we can start to shed unhelpful and painful beliefs.

Projection

In the group home, I enjoyed running something I called a "projection group" with the boys. The idea of projection groups is to inspire in participants a connection to something positive and powerful in themselves. There are a few different versions of this, but all of them have a similar intentions and outcomes. The goal is to create an emotionally provocative way of tapping into the strengths of participants. When it works, the outcome is a sense of empowerment and worthiness.

One version of projection group we would do after the sun went down. In the fall and spring, this did not have to be too late, but there were times I would come home late from work because I was orchestrating a projection group in the early evening. Often it would be encapsulated with other experientially based groups. I and the other staff would take the boys on a hike up a nearby canyon. We hiked to a certain point on the trail where there was a massive cliff face. The top of cliff was about one hundred feet up from the spot we were standing. We would then tell the kids that this evening we were going to conquer that cliff by carefully climbing it. Some kids would be excited, and others would be nervous. After discussing if it would be possible, the group was then handed one rope that they had to hold onto as group. Then they were blindfolded. Lastly, we invited them to be silent throughout the exercise until otherwise instructed.

The staff and I would then lead the group by the rope off the main trail and up a path that was hidden by the cliff face. The path was much easier and more approachable for gaining the top of the cliff. We would lead boys up to the top of the cliff, and then the blindfolds were taken off.

At this point, the boys stood at a high point in the canyon that looked over the city and lake in the valley below. Having completed this activity at night, the sky was filled with millions of stars, and the city was lit up like a reflection of the heavens with tens of thousands of twinkling lights that stretched out across the valley floor. It is one of those spaces whose beauty can suck the air right out of your lungs.

Atop the cliff, after the boys had a moment to soak in the beauty of the vista, they were invited to think about a quality in themselves that they had lost sight of, something that lied within themselves that perhaps they had forgotten, a positive characteristic that is unique to them. We would talk to them about the two most powerful words in the English language: "I am." These words define us for good or for bad. They shape who we are and who we are becoming.

We would explain to the boys that now is as good as any time to take back the identity that we may have lost for a time or buried under the chaos of more recent years. After they thought about what characteristics or qualities they were going to reclaim and own today, we invited them to stand at the peak of the cliff where two perpendicular cliff faces met and projected outwards. I think of it a little bit like Pride Rock from the "Lion King." As the boys stood at this point, they were to project out into the night sky the qualities they were going to reclaim. The staff and I would explain and emphasized the difference between *yelling* and *projecting*. Yelling is loud. Projecting comes from your toes and flows out from the soul. We would tell them that when it is true projection, it will send a chill down the spine of everyone present.

To build their confidence and demonstrate what the expectation looks like, I would often go first. Then they were invited to stand and project one at a time in any order. There were times that one of the boys would standup in that spot and project with such passion that my heartstrings would tear. That type of passion was contagious and got the others excited and pumped up to participate.

Not everyone had that heart-felt, penetrating, soulful projection, but almost always there were at least a few or even a majority of the group who did project. "I AM POWERFUL!" "I AM SMART!" "I AM KIND!" "I AM LOVED!" "I AM LOVING!" Meaningful participation was important because the action of projecting these statements was more than just a cute exercise. Those statements were true. And if the boys could start to feel the words, start to own them, the session could be a game changer

We would also do this during some of our wilderness outings. We would backpack into the backcountry for three days (two nights) once a month through all the warmer months, which usually included more than six months out of the year. In the middle of nowhere and where there was not a soul to be seen, I would start to look for an area that had a nice echo. My favorite spots were often small lakes that had a large cliff rising on the far side. The cliff would echo your words in crisp tones when you projected at it.

If I could find a spot like that, we would all stop and project at the cliff. Each boy would think of some part of himself that needed to be dug back up, something that needed to be reclaim. One of the fun features of these areas is that the echo feedback of a projection is immediate and naturally occurring. If a boy failed to trigger an echo, he would be encouraged to go again. It is a powerful moment when someone initially believes they "can't" make an echo, but with some support and encouragement, it absolutely happens. The Empowerment is a beautiful thing.

This kind of projection group can also be done indoors. I would usually use jimbe drums, but clapping works just as well. Everyone in the group then claps, loudly, two beats at the same time and projects nice and loud, "I AM!" Then one boy in group stood up and projected his statement. We repeated the pattern until everyone had the opportunity to project his own statement. (In group at the facility, I would often go in a circle, but this is not necessary). Each boy was reinforced for participating, and we staff would make a big deal when a projection made our spines tingle. The feedback to the boys was meaningful.

These are three examples of projection group that we would do periodically at the group home. I think it is important to repeatedly challenge the "I'm broken, worthless, or unlovable" templates that are so prevalent for many of us. Projection groups represent one fun way of challenging those templates in a way that is meaningful and empowering. Guided imagery also can be a powerful way of challenging these negative core beliefs.

Eternal Self Template

I use this style of imagery quite frequently, most often with someone who was feeling stuck or not open to ideas. One example of this would be clients that bring their problems to group, only to shut down any and all ideas that people share to help them reframe or cope with the issue. This attitude is a passive way for the person with the problem to put the rest of the group in their place. These clients simply sit back and say something like: "I've already tried that," "I don't think that would work for me," or "no way, I'm not going to do that."

I joke that these clients do not want help with their problems and just wanted to shoot clay pigeons. They would sit comfortably in their chair with their shotgun, and no matter what came out of anyone's mouth they could just look that direction and shoot the idea down. Blowing up the clay pigeon and leaving a dirty mess in their wake while they just hung out and enjoyed the fruits of their labor. I would not use guided imagery in a group setting, but could circle back around to it in individual therapy when I see this dynamic going on in group.

There are two important concepts I would like to communicate as we dive into the concept of the eternal self: it can be a great substitute for Divinity when a client has no equivalent belief or is otherwise uncomfortable with the idea of a Divine.

If I have a client that I know has issues with the concept of a Higher Power, I am not going to include it in his or her therapy. In place of the Higher Power in the typical template, I would start the same by having the client connect with people that have his or her best interest at heart, asking, "Do you love me?" but then I would have the client imagine his or her "Eternal Self" (instead of a Higher Power) steps forward from the group of people and ask that Eternal Self, "Do you love me?"

So in place of trying to convince a client to use some coping skill or trying to teach something new, it would be an opportunity to do an imagery. As is the case in all these templates, I set up by stating, "Imagine a group of people that has your best interest at heart. They can be alive or dead, known or unknown, anyone throughout all humanity but they must have this one thing in common, your best interest at heart. Once you can see them in your mind's eye, I want you to ask that group of people, Do you love me? And feel the response! Then I want you to imagine that from among this group of people that has your best interest at heart steps forward your Higher Power. Whatever that looks like to you, and ask the same question: Do you love me? And feel the response!"

In this case, I used the Higher Power because my assumption is that the individual is not averse to such, and so I am not using the Eternal Self as a substitute for the Divine. Once these foundations are laid, I would then invite the client to imagine his or her Eternal Self: "Now I want you to imagine your Eternal Self also steps out from the crowd. This is not who you are today, but that part of you that existed before you were born and will exist afterwards. This is like the best part of you, not someone that you would like to be in the future, or the *potential* you, but the person you really are at the core, that innocent, loving, curious, powerful part of you that is left when you wipe away all the debris and craziness of this life."

"I want you to have a conversation with your Eternal Self. Describe the problems you are facing and all the many roadblocks in the way. Take as much time as you want, and let me know when finished." Then I wait.

Once the client gives the go ahead, I say, "Ask your Eternal Self for three things to do this week to help to get over your current challenges. Take as much time as you need." And then I wait again. When the client gives the go ahead, I will usually ask them if he or she wants to share the three strategies that were mentioned. In these type of imagery, clients share the information much more frequently than in the more personal trauma-type imageries. If the client chooses not to share the three points, it is not a big deal; I then simply move to closing. If he or she tells me the three things to do during the established time period, write the items for the client to help him or her remember

When I move to close the imagery, I usually say, "Now give a big hug to your Eternal Self. Tell your Eternal Self anything that you want, and listen to whatever that Self wants to tell you." After a pause, I let the client know to open his or her eyes when ready.

It has never ceased to amaze me how easily this technique moves someone from being closed to new possibilities, to open. It is important not to be defensive if some of the suggestions are something that you gave to them at some point or that were encouraged during a group session. The important piece is not where the idea came from but the buy-in of the individual when the client feels like he or she has control to accept or reject the suggestions. Having the suggestion come from themselves makes it much more difficult to reject.

Apollo Jize

Sometimes it is easier to remain stuck in the holes we dig for ourselves than to climb our way out of them. I have a therapist friend who likes to say, Is that a pit or a pinecone?" Some people treat setbacks like sitting in a pit of despair where one wallows in self-pity, hate, revenge fantasies, depression and anxiety. Others treat setbacks like sitting on a ponderosa pinecone, which are large and spiked and very unpleasant to sit on. It gets them moving, immediately!

I remember a young boy that was having one of "those weeks." He felt like nothing was going his way, and in truth, he was facing some really hard situations. He had just learned over a phone call that his parents were getting divorced. He had a confrontation with staff that went south, which they both could have handled better. He had become very belligerent and said some insulting and mean things in both situations. This was quite peculiar for him, as usually he was respectful, hardworking, and responsibly engaged in treatment and in the group home.

In session he seemed to be in a loop, reinforcing his negative self-talk and struggling to see a purpose and a way forward. As we were talking, the idea to work through an imagery came to mind. I asked him, "Are you okay if we do something a bit weird?" He consented, so we began. He closed his eyes, and we both took a few cleansing breaths. "Imagine a group of people that has your best interest at heart. These people could be alive or dead, known or unknown, anyone throughout all eternity, but they must have your best interest at heart." Pause. "Once you can see that group of people gathered in your mind's eye, ask them this one question: Do you love me? And then feel the response!" Pause. "Next, imagine that from among this group of people that have your best interest at heart stepped forward your Higher Power. Connect with that Divine Entity, that Power, that Love, that Universal Cosmically Involved Being. And ask the same question: Do you love me? And feel the response!"

Apollo Jize seemed to be in a good place just walking through these two steps. He seemed more relaxed and centered. The room felt palpably different than it had just moments earlier when it had been filled with so much hate and pain. I said to him, "Imagine that from among that group of people stepped forward your Eternal Self, that part of yourself that transcends the misery of this life and the current moment, that is outside of the emotional conflicts and games of your parents, that has a more eternal and cosmic view of things."

Once he indicated he had pulled this up in his mind's eye, I continued: "With your Eternal Self in front of you, talk to him about all of the frustrations and problems of the week. Put everything on the table. Take as much time as you need, and let me know when you are done." We sat in silence for a good ten minutes or so before he signaled. I told him, "Ask your Eternal Self for three things you can do this week to pull yourself, if not out of the mire, through it. Listen to what your Eternal Self tells you to do, and let me know when you are done."

After almost no time, he stated they were done. When I asked Apollo if he wanted to share what he had learned, he stated that he was told one word three times: apologize.

We then concluded the imagery. "I want you to thank your Eternal Self for being there for you. Wrap him up in a big hug. Tell him anything that you feel inspired to say, and listen to anything that your Eternal Self wanted to tell you. Then when you are ready, open your eyes."

While discussing the experience, Apollo initially complained about the instruction he received, but he relented that he would follow through with the commitment that he made to his Eternal Self. Apollo told me that despite not wanting to do it and feeling he was justified in his anger, he knew that he should not lash out and act it out as he had before and that in his heart of hearts, he knew that he was wrong. He was committed to following through.

Conclusion

Because Eternal Self imagery is so client-centered, it has a strong empowering effect on clients. If anyone were to suggest to Apollo to apologize, he would have responded defensively. But in this scenario, despite his own reluctance, because drawing on the inner wisdom of his Eternal Self is very non-threatening, he was able to take a new perspective and therefore new action toward resolving his problems.

Because of the flexibility of the intervention, it can be repeated with the same client with new results each time. As in all imagery work, this template should be used moderately; you just want this template to be one of the many interventions in your back of tricks.

Sometimes it is helpful to write down any goals/interventions clients are given so they can reference them over the next week or so. Remember to keep the time periods reasonable, and ideally the goals are something that can be measurable. That stated, these are not SMART goals (Simple, Measurable, Achievable, Realistic, and Timely), and therefore there will be times they are fairly abstract. To allow for the client process, you should avoid shaping the goals to fit a specific model. Just let the process grow organically from the experience.

The power of this intervention is the way it helps someone to recognize that he or she is not an ugly duckling, but a beautiful swan. And that swan gives great advice. Trust the process, ride the wave, and see where it takes your client. Be a spectator in the transformation.

Eternal Self Template

- Imagine a group of people that has your best interest at heart. They can be alive or dead, known or unknown, anyone throughout all humanity but they must have this one thing in common, your best interest at heart. Once you can see them in your mind's eye, I want you to ask that group of people, Do you love me? And feel the response!

- Then I want you to imagine that from among this group of people that has your best interest at heart steps forward your Higher Power. Whatever that looks like to you, and ask the same question: Do you love me? And feel the response!

- Now I want you to imagine your Eternal Self also steps from the crowd. This is not who you are today, but that part of you that existed before you were born and will exist afterwards. This is like the best part of you, not someone that you would like to be in the future, or the *potential* you, but the person you really are at the core, that innocent, loving, curious, powerful part of you that is left when you wipe away all the debris and craziness of this life.

- I want you to have a conversation with your Eternal Self. Describe the problems you are facing and all the many roadblocks in the way. Take as much time as you want, and let me know when you're finished.

- Ask your Eternal Self for three things to do this week to help to get over your current challenges. Take as much time as you need

- Do you want to share the three strategies that were mentioned?

- Now give a big hug to your Eternal Self. Tell your Eternal Self anything that you want and listen to whatever that Self wants to tell you.

- When you are ready, open your eyes and come back to this space.

GOD SHOPPING

Fast Food

My daughter is a university student and works a student job at a fast-food joint on campus. I frequently hear her work sagas, and one recurring character is an unreliable coworker. According to my daughter, he "never" shows up to work on time. He also commits to cover shifts for others and then "forgets." Apparently, this type of behavior happens on regular bases.

Having been in a supervisory role in the past, this surprised me. When I was residential director of a local group home, if I had someone no-show, that was typically grounds for dismissal, even if it was the first time. If a person was generally a good employee and the miss was highly out of character the instance may pass the first time with a formal warning. Even under those circumstances, if the situation was to repeat itself, the person would inevitably be terminated. A third absence—let alone a fourth or fifth like my daughter's coworker—would not be an option.

From the time my daughter had started work (about eight months ago), the joint had never been fully staffed. She explained that they could not get rid of a worker even if his or her performance was subpar. In addition, this young man is fairly good-natured and a favorite of the manager, which, my daughter believes, further protects the young man.

One of the interesting features of her experience, though, is that this dysfunctional dynamic is self-reinforcing through fear. The system is not optimal, but because the fear of the unknown, there is a paralyzing effect that stifles progress (ex. getting rid of problematic employees). It is like they say, the devil you know is better than the devil you don't know.

SBNR (spiritual but not religious)

One of the hang-ups that I have had people articulate to me about guided imagery in the way we have been discussing is the idea that there is an imposition of belief onto others. I think one of the concerns people have that are of specific faith traditions is they do not want to impose their religious views and beliefs onto others. It is unethical for a practitioner to shape therapy by the clinician's own belief system

That stated, I do not believe that the style of imagery that we have been discussing here imposes a specific template for the Divine or imposes a religious expectation. In this era of texting, memes, and messenger, I have found that my kids have become fonder of acronyms than your average therapist (and that is hard to do because we pack as much as we can into short letter combinations). One I have been recently exposed to was SBNR, spiritual but not religious.

God Shopping

I like that concept. I believe that there is a difference between being spiritual and being religious. I am certainly not an expert in this area, but let me lay out what I see as the difference between the two. Religiousness is a connection and participation in some form of organized and formal practice that facilitates a relationship with the Divine. Religion is typically accompanied by specific systems of belief and has a defined Deity that has a name or label. There is often leadership that both teaches and monitors adherence (to some degree) to specific dogma and doctrine.

Spirituality is amorphous and personal. There are no specific requirements or practices that come with spirituality. It is a personal feeling of connection with something bigger than oneself. This can include a specific Deity that is embedded in formal religion, but it can also be any connection beyond oneself. Spirituality is defined and approached from an introspective place.

In the Alcoholics Anonymous Big Book, there is a chapter entitled "We Agnostics" (N/A, 1939)." This chapter does a great job exploring the bristling effect that conversations about God and religion have on many people. The book also acknowledges that for the miracle of healing to transpire, a seeker must become willing to acknowledge that something is out there greater than him or herself, sometimes that has his or her best interest at heart and has the power to enact miracles—even to change hearts.

Like in AA, guided imagery works best when including a Higher Power, and the Divine serves as a spiritual framework for clients of all beliefs to fill in as they see best. There are people that find religion to be a conduit and connecting power to the Divine. In these cases, religion fosters and nurtures spirituality. But to others, religion feels oppressive and stifling and the lists of do's and don'ts become an impediment to finding meaningful connection with God. In these situations, religion gets in the way of spirituality. At the end of the day, each of us should be in the driver's seat as to if and how religion and spirituality come together or diverge in our own life. As a clinician, the goal is to provide a safe, accepting place where the client's experience (or lack thereof) of the Divine is respected and, when appropriate, fostered.

That is where the concept of *God shopping* comes in. This imagery is not concerned with religion. In other words, this imagery is not *religion* shopping; it is shaping the conceptualization that a person might have of the Divine.

Some peoples' experience with their Higher Powers is very similar to my daughter's experience with her coworker. My daughter's coworker was unreliable, but he was socially established, and the system seemingly had no better alternative. Similarly, some people feel stuck with an unreliable Divinity that is socially established by family or culture, and there seems to be no better alternative in which to place hope

There are times where attending meetings and seeing friends have social advantages even if the practice itself feels hollow. It is possible there are times we hold on to the concept of our Higher Power as we know them just because we are afraid that there will be an emptiness and void remaining. Maybe we have been so socially indoctrinated that we fear divine retribution for questioning dogma. At the end of the day, the devil you know is better than the devil you don't.

The purpose and goal of this guided imagery intervention is to play with concepts of the Divine in what can be a non-threatening, and even fun, manner. We simply start by firing God.

God Shopping Template

To make this intervention effective, the client must have full constructive power when reimagining God. Clinician are to guide the process but is *not* to shaping the outcome. The goal is to allow the clients to redefine their conception of a Higher Power and in so doing change their relationship with that Divine.

Previously I made mention of the philosopher Friedrich Nietzsche and the influence he had on Freud. Let me quote one of his more famous passages so we see the context in which the "God is dead" comment was made. This is known as the parable of "The Madman" from *The Joyful Wisdom* (Nietzsche, 1910):

> Have you not heard of that madman who lit a lantern in the bright morning hours, ran to the market-place, and cried incessantly: "I am looking for God! I am looking for God!" As many of those who did not believe in God were standing together there, he excited considerable laughter. Have you lost him, then? Said one. Did he lose his way like a child? Said another. Or is he hiding? Is he afraid of us? Has he gone on a voyage? Or emigrated? Thus they shouted and laughed. The madman sprang into their midst and pierced them with his glances.
>
> "Where has God gone?" he cried. "I shall tell you. We have killed him - you and I. We are his murderers. But how have we done this? How were we able to drink up the sea? Who gave us the sponge to wipe away the entire horizon? What did we do when we unchained the earth from its sun? Whither is it moving now? Whither are we moving now? Away from all suns? Are we not perpetually falling? Backward,

sideward, forward, in all directions? Is there any up or down left? Are we not straying as through an infinite nothing? Do we not feel the breath of empty space? Has it not become colder? Is it not more and more night coming on all the time? Must not lanterns be lit in the morning? Do we not hear anything yet of the noise of the gravediggers who are burying God? Do we not smell anything yet of God's decomposition? Gods too decompose. God is dead. God remains dead. And we have killed him. How shall we, murderers of all murderers, console ourselves? That which was the holiest and mightiest of all that the world has yet possessed has bled to death under our knives. Who will wipe this blood off us? With what water could we purify ourselves? What festivals of atonement, what sacred games shall we need to invent? Is not the greatness of this deed too great for us? Must we not ourselves become gods simply to be worthy of it? There has never been a greater deed; and whosoever shall be born after us - for the sake of this deed he shall be part of a higher history than all history hitherto."

Here the madman fell silent and again regarded his listeners; and they too were silent and stared at him in astonishment. At last he threw his lantern to the ground, and it broke and went out. "I have come too early," he said then; "my time has not come yet. The tremendous event is still on its way, still travelling - it has not yet reached the ears of men. Lightning and thunder require time, the light of the stars requires time, deeds require time even after they are done, before they can be seen and heard. This deed is still more distant from them than the distant stars - and yet they have done it themselves."

These passages are quite thick, and I will not pretend to be a philosopher with keen insight to there meanings, but one of the discernable concepts is the idea that we, humanity, have lost sight of God. We have forgotten and ridiculed God and made God into something to be mocked and derided. Then there is this lament about the cold void that is the byproduct of relinquishing a belief in God and the uncertainty that comes from that space.

Now, there are many people that feel comfortable not believing in God. This too is an option and should not be the target of intervention. This process is for those that do have a belief in the Divine and desire connection but feel abandoned and ignored by God. For these people, sometimes the process of finding new meaning in their Higher Power can be empowering. It can inspire healing and transcendent meaning. Such cognitive-spiritual shifts can provide meaning and purpose to people and support the healing process. Therefore, reconnecting with the Divine can be powerful medicine to those that suffer.

The proposition of this intervention is not to "kill God" per se, but it is to redefine what one's Higher Power is and how that Power manifests in one's own life. Life is extremely complicated and riddled with both uncertainty and inexplicable suffering. These dynamics can challenge the development and trust in a loving Higher Power that watches over, cares about, and has our best interest at heart. The goal of God shopping is to move from a subconscious projection of the Divine to a conscious creation of a God worthy of being worshiped.

As with all the templates we have discussed, I set up the imagery the way we usually do. I ask my client to close his or her eyes and take a few calming breaths. We practice this a few times together. Then I say, "Imagine a group of people that have your best interest at heart. They can be alive or dead, known or unknown, anyone throughout all humanity but they must have your best interest at heart. Then ask this group of people with your best interest at heart, Do you love me? And feel the response!

"Now imagine that from among that group of people that have your best interest at heart steps forward your Higher Power, God, Krishna, Mother Nature, the Universe, whatever that looks like to you. And I want you to ask that being, that essence, that power, Do you love me? And feel the response!"

At this stage, while their eyes are closed, I describe the concept of a *pink slip*. "In some companies, when someone is underperforming or when his or her position is no longer needed, the employee receive a 'pink slip' that informs them that they are fired. Imagine a personal mailbox, like a PO box in a line of mailboxes, with personal keys to get the mail from each box. If someone were to be fired, he or she would find a pink slip of paper in the mailbox giving the date of his or her last day of work. Termination could be immediate, in a few days, or in a few weeks; but the decision has already been made. We are going to take one of these pink slips and put it into God's mailbox. He just has not been showing up. He has not played his role as protector."

I usually pull from the client's language and his or her concept of a Higher Power, including role expectations, titles, and pronouns. As in all imagery, the clinician should always be in the background and not in the driver's seat. Sometimes I have the client imagine being present when God find's the pink slip so the client can witness God's reaction to being fired. For some clients, witnessing God's reaction can be empowering as they retake a sense of control. But for more empathic people they may not want to hurt someone else and it would be better to not emphasize an eye witness perspective.

"Our next step is to set up a 'help wanted ad' for a new Higher Power. In the ad, you should include all the things that you have needed of God that the fired God did not historically provide. You can list these things off verbally, or you can just think of them in your mind and let me know when you are ready to move forward."

Next, I typically walk the client through a hiring process. "Imagine a line of three to five God candidates waiting nervously in a hall to be interviewed. Bring them in one at a time and talk to them about their qualifications, their strengths and weaknesses, etc. Let me know when you have completed all the interviews." Once the client has completed the interview process, he or she is free to either higher one of the prospective candidates, draw up a new ad using the information learned thus far, and then cycle through the interview process again.

This goes on until the client has found the perfect candidate, a candidate that the client can love and from whom he or she can feel loved, a candidate that cares and listens, or whatever criteria the client had established for the God he or she needs in life. "Now I want you to imagine wrapping this newly hired Devine in a hug. Thank them for their willingness to be there for you. Listen to anything they might have to say." Pause. "When you are ready you can open your eyes and join me back in this space."

Now this can feel like walking a fine line. I would not intend for the experience to be flippant or disrespectful. The goal is not to focus on specific organized religions and systems of theology. This is simply an interactive process of finding a God that will show up and support the client in the way that they need in order to reciprocate the relationship with their Higher Power.

Dee Ose

There is a difficult dynamic that can sometimes play out with kids in the group home when one of parents have been sexually abused themselves. When I have worked in family systems where the parents are emotionally distant and even hostile towards the boy in our group home, there seems to be a high correlation between that and one of the parents having been the victim of sexual violence themselves, often through being abused by a family member.

In those situations, the parent's personal trauma gets tied up in the horror of learning of their own children's victimization and even more difficult when his or her own child was the instigator of the abuse. Sometimes I call this the "schizophrenia of incestual sexual abuse." The parents are concerned and want to protect the victim that is their child. And they are super upset about the abuse that was perpetrated by one of their other children. Yet, there is also a protective instinct towards the child that offended. They want them to get help, but not necessarily be vilified in the criminal system.

As previously stated, sometimes in situations where one of the parents have their own history of being sexually victimized these dynamics get slightly altered. The dynamics shift and the protective piece for the child that perpetrated the abuse evaporates. This is not universally true, as few things are when it comes to human interactions, but it is a dynamic I see often when the parent is more focused on the justice side of the equation vs. the mercy. Just to clarify this is not a critique of such reactions. I don't believe there is a right way or a wrong way to feel when being presented with the nightmare of learning sexual abuse has occurring between one's own children. I do take exceptions to responses that include physical violence, but the feelings themselves are what they are.

During one of the wilderness trips with the young men from the group home, one of the boys was quite the talker. He was not my personal client, but I did work in group with him. As we were trekking along, he liked to stay close to me and chat about a broad array of topics. He was bright and had a lot of interesting perspectives, even if I thought some of them might be a bit off the beaten path.

This young man, whom we will call Dee Ose, came from a highly conservative religious family. He however frequently explored ideas from diverse religious traditions outside of those promoted by his family of origin. I believe this was in part an attempt to rebel against his parents. His relationship with them was very tenuous. This predated his sexual offending behavior but was certainly exacerbated by those choices.

Several months before the trek, I had referenced in group that my grandmother was Wiccan. During the wilderness trip, Dee Ose tried to scour the recesses of my mind about Wicca. The reality is that I did not know a lot about what my grandmother practiced or believed other than basic beliefs in the five elements and some karmic-like principles of what goes around comes around.

Not surprisingly, a few days later when I visited Dee for a therapy session at the end of his solo experience, he was interested in talking about religion. In place of an intellectual-factual conversation about religions, which is where we had spent his time talking over the last few days while hiking, we decided to do guided imagery to explore the experience of God more directly.

It started out under the usual umbrella: "Imagine a group of people that have your best interest at heart. Alive or dead, known or unknown, anyone throughout all humanity, but they must have this one common interest: your best interest at heart. When they have gathered in your mind's eye, I want you to ask them, Do you love me? And feel the response." Pause. Then even though he was conflicted about God, we did the connecting with the Divine piece: "Imagine that from among the people that have your best interest at heart steps forward your Higher Power, whatever that looks like to you, and ask the same question: Do you love me? And feel the response." Pause.

At this point, we began the God shopping template. "We were going to fill out a pink slip for the God that never showed up for you, the one that you are frustrated with. Delineate in your mind's eye all the reason that you cannot trust or work with that God anymore."

In this case, he did not do the imagery in silence but chose to articulate his complaints out loud. He mentioned several different ways that God failed to show up. "When I was little, I had been taught that I could pray and God would listen; but when I prayed that my parents would stop fighting or get divorced, neither ever happened. There were times I could hear my father yelling at the top of his lungs at my mom, and I would hide in the basement with my siblings and try to entertain and distract them from the mess that was going on upstairs. My parents were highly involved in their religious community, and it was not uncommon that the next day after a fight the family would all get dressed up in our fine clothing, put on a smile, and go to church where everything seemed just fine.

"I came to question the plastic smiles and kindness of everyone in his church. I could not help but wonder how many other moms were being beaten and violated by their husbands. I wondered how many of the other kids in the church hid somewhere in their homes hoping the parental storm would pass."

These experiences reinforced a certain cynicism that colored Dee Ose's entire religious experience. The combination of feeling like his prayers were empty words and that people were shells of fake smiles and mock happiness convinced him that God simply did not care about him or about humans in general. And a God that did not care was not someone he was going to spend time worshipping.

Dee Ose's complaints and experiences came pouring out in a flood of words and emotion. Once he cleared his system of his complaints, I told him, "You needed to summarize all of that on a pink piece of paper in your mind's eye. When you're done, flip over the page and in big, bold letters write, 'You're fired.'"

I asked Dee, "Would you prefer to put the pink slip into God's mail box or deliver it in person?" Dee wanted to put it into his box. So, we imagined a group of mail boxes to all sorts of people, and one of them had "God" printed on it. When we found God's box, we simply deposited the pink slip. I then invited Dee to put out a help wanted ad. "Think about what you would need in a God that you could feel comfortable with and get behind."

Dee Ose listed off several things. "At the top of my list, I want someone to hear me when I pray. And not just to be heard, but heard by someone that could show they were listening. I want a Higher Power that cares and is invested in my life and future, that is concerned for my well-being both physically and emotionally. I want a God that was not afraid of science and that let me think for myself." There were many other features Dee listed that have faded from my mind, but he listed out all the qualities he needed in a God he would be willing to believe in.

We posted this in the *Universe Post*, a newspaper that all the Gods subscribe to. We went into some detail about how he wanted it to be printed. If it was embedded in all the other adds or if he wanted it to be front page news. He decided he wanted it to be listed with all the other ads. "I don't want it to stand out and be significant; I wanted any Gods that responds to have had to searched for the ad; these Gods are not going to show up because the ad was thrown in their faces but because they wanted to find someone they could help—they wanted to find and help me."

After entering the ad, I guided him, "Imagine that you get a smattering of responses, and you set up a day for interviews. Each of the Gods are to be brought in one at a time to talk with you. You can ask them anything you want, and you are to pay attention to both what they each say and the way each act." This part he did in silence and in his own head, but the results of this version were entertaining. When the first Divinity came in for an interview, as we sat in silence, Dee had tears that dripped down his cheek. I had told him to let me know when he was done and to take as much time as he liked. When he said he was good, I told him to invite in the next God. Dee shook his head. "No. I've already hired the first God. He is perfect."

I asked Dee if he wanted me to shoo off the rest or if he wanted me to let them know that he had already hired someone. He said he wanted to take care of it. He told me that he walked out into the lobby of his image and addressed the applicants, thanking them for coming and letting them know that he had already decided who to hire.

God Shopping

Dee Ose afterwards described having been swept with an overwhelming sense of love and connection as he interviewed his first God candidate. Dee said he felt liberated in firing the detached, vengeful God of his past and looked forward to the relationship with this new Divinity.

Dee moved from residential setting to proctor care and continued to live within the umbrella of our system for another eighteen months after this imagery session. His connection to the new Divinity never did fade even when things did not go well for him and when he was unable to return home the way he had hoped.

That is not to say that such an experience will be universal, but in this case study there seemed to be a mutual understanding between Dee and his Divinity that they were both imperfect and would love and accept one another come what may. Dee felt like his prayers were heard, and he felt personally connected to his concept of the Divine. Dee said this was a pivotal moment in his recovery where he felt totally loved and accepted for who he is, despite the failures of his past. That unconditional positive regard that he felt from the God of his own creation became a template for getting past shame and self-loathing that had plagued his past.

Conclusion

God Shopping becomes a way of redefining one's relationship with the Divine, and often embedded in this shift will also be greater self-acceptance. The potential problem with a newly hired God is that inevitably there will still be times when prayers are not answered and bad things happen. I remember feeling anxious about the inevitable disillusion that people would experience when their new Gods didn't answer prayers the way the clients wanted. I have yet had that fear materialize. No one has ever articulated being let down by the new Divine they hired in their imagery.

I hope from what has been described you can see the difference between addressing questions about religion (dogma, practice, systems, etc.), and that of questioning the God they have experienced. The God of a client's creation can plug into a religious system if that is what works for them, or the God can be an independent source of spirituality. The exact permutations of that dynamic are not important to me as a clinician; what is important is that the client takes control of shedding unhelpful or harmful beliefs about God (uncaring, vengeful, distant, judgmental) with healing and powerful beliefs about the Divine (loving, merciful, patient).

For some people, it may not be helpful or necessary to replace the dysfunction of their God. For some people, the rational approach that discards the metaphysical for observable reality can be just as effective. The most important concept in this template is to get rid of belief systems that reinforce shame and keep people stuck. This template is meant to be a highly liberating experience.

God Shopping

God Shopping Template

- Imagine a group of people that have your best interest at heart. They can be alive or dead, known or unknown, anyone throughout all humanity but they must have their best interest at heart. Then ask this group of people with your best interest at heart, Do you love me? And feel the response!

- Now imagine that from among that group of people that have your best interest at heart steps forward your Higher Power, God, Krishna, Mother Nature, the Universe, whatever that looks like to you. And I want you to ask that being, that essence, that power, Do you love me? And feel the response!

- In some companies, when someone is underperforming or when his or her position is no longer needed, the employee receive a 'pink slip' that informs them that they are fired. Imagine a personal mailbox, like a PO box in a line of mailboxes, with personal keys to get the mail from each box. If someone were to be fired, he or she would find a pink slip of paper in the mailbox giving the date of his or her last day of work. Termination could be immediate, in a few days, or in a few weeks; but the decision has already been made. We are going to take one of these pink slips and put it into God's mailbox. He just has not been showing up. He has not played his role as protector.

- Our next step is to set up a help wanted ad for a new Higher Power. In the ad, you should include all the things that you have needed of God that the fired God did not historically provide. You can list these things off verbally, or you can just think of them in your mind and let me know when you are ready to move forward.

- Imagine a line of three to five God candidates waiting nervously in a hall to be interviewed. Bring them in one at a time and talk to them about their qualifications, their strengths and weaknesses, etc. Let me know when you have completed all the interviews.
- Now I want you to imagine wrapping this newly hired Devine in a hug. Thank them for their willingness to be there for you. Listen to anything they might have to say.
- When you are ready you can open your eyes and join me back in this space.

GRIEF

Media

Over the years, it has become a running joke with my kids that when we are watching a movie, if someone kills or kidnaps a family member of the star of the show, I will turn to my kids and say something like, "Uh oh, he should not have done that. Now he is going to pay." The kids giggle, knowing the familiar trope often set up in movies, books, and plays. The protagonist witnesses the death of a loved one and then seeks revenge, bringing the antagonist to justice (and often in vigilante style).

Hollywood is chuck-full of these types of movies including some of my favorites: *Braveheart*, *The Patriot*, *Gladiator*, *The Crow*, *The Professional*, and *Desperado* are just a few classics from my childhood. Although this makes for great media, often in real life, the grief that comes with the loss of a loved one can have serious and long-term psychological consequences on survivors.

Guilt seems to be deeply connected to grief. For example, many women who miscarry blame their diet or exercise for the miscarriage; they can become self-deprecating and struggle to grasp the often uncontrollability and unpredictability of biology. This conflict can also be seen in the death of loved ones, divorce, wayward children, etc. Knowing these facts does not ease the pain of the mind that is always searching to identify meaning and causation.

People by nature are meaning-making mammals. It is the reason that things such as astrology and tarot readings can be so impactful. The cerebral cortex was developed to extract inferences and connect meaning to presupposed randomness. Therefore, despite knowing a specific pair of socks does not have magical properties that increase the probability of winning a basketball game, it is not uncommon that some article of clothing or ritual becomes a psychological aid in laying the foundations for success. For many people attributing guilt to themselves or some behavior they have performed fills that need to find meaning in the random chaos of life.

In the face of death, we often see this in the denial that can become so entrenched in the initial disclosure of death. Someone might say, "He couldn't die in a car accident. I was talking with him this morning on the phone and everything was fine." There may be an emotional reaction where they believe the person is still alive despite all evidence to the contrary, and the person becomes upset with medical professionals for not recognizing that his or her loved one can still recover. This hope beyond hope drives decisions to keep people on life supporting technology long after recovery has any probability.

Grief

On a personal note, I remember when my maternal grandmother was on the decline (physically and mentally). Initially the family was taking care of her in the home. Grandpa did as much as he could to attend to her needs. There were professional hospice workers in the home regularly. Over about three years, the family was periodically called together for their last goodbyes. We would receive a tearful phone call describing grandma passing through phases of incoherence and brief moments of recognition, and everyone was certainty she would pass within hours. This emotional yo-yo was very difficult for everyone. The urgency of these calls was received with more and more skepticism

My grandmother eventually was moved to a facility and lingered in that place for years. When I would visit her, grandma often complained about her inability to die. To make meaning of her situation, she told herself that she was being punished by God for something, and that if she could only identify a particular sin or transgression, she would be released from the pain. After being bed ridden in a state of utter vulnerability for years was taxing on her. And these conversations with her were emotionally taxing on me.

Eventually I stopped visiting as regular. Then, she died. I was asked to speak at her funeral, and I remember feeling so conflicted. I felt guilty that I had not seen her in so long. Part of me was in denial that she would ever pass, and most of that was self-protection from the emotional toll that these interactions had on me. I thought it was selfish of me, and I felt extremely guilty.

A few years earlier, I had spent time collecting stories from grandma that I put together in a biography. This was distributed to each of her five kids and some of the older grandchildren. I know grandma knew that I loved her, and yet

I could not shake the feeling of negligence on my part as I prepared to speak at the funeral.

For the most part, death is untimely. Even when it feels like a good thing, like releasing my grandmother from constant pain and intellectual fog. There remains a propensity to *should on ourselves*. The list of "I should have done" can be endless and perpetual, and yet the surviving loved ones need a way to move forward.

The ritualization of death through funerals, memorials, burials, urns, etc. is an important part of the healing process for many. The reminiscing and stories can bring great healing. My maternal grandfather died about a year after grandma. After his passing, we were cleaning out their house and ran into boxes of pictures. One of the most healing moments in the loss of my grandparents was sitting around with my aunts, uncles, and cousins going through old photos and telling stories. "Do you remember when . . ." became like a healing balm to my grieving soul.

Grief Template

Grief does not have to come from death specifically. It is common to grieve all sorts of things. This often can include the loss of a vision of the future that one had played out in his or her own mind. Parents getting divorce changes the perceived stability and future of a family; sometimes this creates emotional trauma in children that later struggle to attach and commit in their own relationships. Parents that are not able to raise a child may choose to adopt to another family more capable of providing the care their child needs; this is a loving act, but there remains a grief for parents (and often for the child) around the experience of "what could have been."

Grief

I have a friend who became pregnant as a teenager and lovingly chose to adopt the child to others. That was over twenty years ago. To this day, she celebrates the child's birthday. When she sees young adults, she reminisces on what her now young-adult child might look like and might be doing at this stage in life. Is her child now married and having grandchildren she will never meet? Is her child successful? and happy? The questions are endless, but the answers are wanting.

There are times that guided imagery can be a powerful way of interacting with grief. Memory is malleable. As we access memories, we change memories. At the end of the day, a common theme of therapy regardless of the approach or philosophy is to change the relationship people have with their own narratives, the stories they tell themselves about their past. In other words, we facilitate the renegotiation of memories.

Imagery can take a very direct approach to this problem. In addition to what I am about to describe, I would encourage people to ritualize dealing with grief. Allow the client room to be inventive and create rituals that may be healing to them. Like all imagery work I have been describing thus far, this is just one tool in the tool belt, not the tool belt.

The set up may go something like this. Someone is soldiering on by him or herself through a circumstance, relationship, death of a loved one, or other painful experience. I will say to them something like, "Do you want to try something weird? Close your eyes and take a few deep cleansing breaths in sync with me. Then, imagine a group of people that have your best interest at heart. They can be alive or dead, known or unknown, anyone throughout all humanity but they must share this one thing in common, your best interest. When you can see that group of people in your mind's eye, let me know somehow. Grunt, thumbs up, whatever, just let me know they are there."

Once the client indicates he or she has them gathered in their mind, I continue: "Now as you look over that group of people that have your best interest at heart, I want you to ask them this questions, Do you love me? And feel the response!" Pause. "Now I want you to imagine that from among this group of people that has your best interest at heart steps forward your Higher Power. Vishnu, Buddha, Mother Earth, Christ; whatever that looks like to you. I want you to connect with that being, that essence, and ask the same question, Do you love me? And feel the response." Pause.

At this point I move into the grief work. Now there are some things that I would encourage you to keep in mind as we move into this phase. If your client has a traumatic memory such as witnessing death in an accident, they may have strong visual images of death. It would be important to do trauma imagery work as found in chapter 6 prior to the grief imagery work presented in this chapter. Nevertheless, there are times that the grief work will transpire prior to other trauma work. It is important to be careful about the images and language used for setting this up based on the client's experience with the death (or other grievous circumstances), which can even include the trauma that sometimes comes by seeing a loved one embalmed in a casket. Anyways, in short, be careful to use positive healing ichnography. This example will focus on death as the form of grief work, but it could just as easily be focused on a wide variety of life experiences, from a sports injury, divorce, rejection from specific school or work situation, etc.

One way to create this is to say something like, "I want you to imagine the Eternal Self of your loved one. Not that part of the person that grew old and died [or whatever the circumstance may have been], but that part of him or her that existed before they were born and continues to exist afterwards. Invite that Eternal Self to have a conversation with you. Let me know when he or she is present."

Like previous imageries we have discussed, you will give only limited direction and just set the stage for the imagery to play out on its own. I typically say, "Take a minute to catch the person up on your life. Let them know about how it felt when he or she died and the challenges that came with adjusting to a life without him or her. Talk to the person about your successes and the awesome things that have happened in your life afterward and about the hard times and struggles. Take as long as you need. Let me know when you are done." Pause. This can be one of those very long pauses. It is not uncommon it will go on for five to ten minutes. Tears are also common.

After the client acknowledges he or she has caught up with the person, I say, "Tell your loved one whatever it is you wished you had time to say before they died [or left], the phrases that have floated around your head and you wished you had only taken the time to say. And then listen to what your person wants to tell you. Take as long as you need. Let me know when you're done."

There may be other instructions I would add, especially if the client did not seem to take much time thinking through the scenario in his or her mind. I may add other prompts as they come to my mind. But, that is all there is to the basic structure. After this is completed, I would close: "Now, give your loved one a hug. Let your love for him or her be known. Whisper it into his or her ear and tell the person anything else you feel would be important. Then listen to what he or she has to tell you. Take as long as you want. When you are ready, just open your eyes and come back into this space."

Grief

Following the imagery, you can check in. Ask the client if he or she wants to share about the experience. Ask if he or she is doing ok. And then work towards closure of the session.

I will give two examples of this type of imagery. The first is a fairly traditional approach, similar to what was just described. The other was an atypical example used to illustrate flexibility. There is no "right way" to do this. It is important to be intuitively present and to follow thoughts and impressions that come during the process; don't be rigid about any specific template.

Stie Fold

There are many versions of grief stories that I have heard over the years, but one that has stuck out a bit more vivid happened to a young man we will call Stie Fold. Stie was in his mid-twenties and had struggled for many years with a heroin addiction that had almost taken his life on several occasions. He had been in treatment on several previous occasions trying to place his life on a new trajectory, but unfortunately it had never been successful.

On his first day of treatment with me, he said that he felt like he had never "dealt with" the death of his father. Stie's father was an addict, and his mother was mostly absent. Growing up as a young man, Stie only had consistent contact was with his father. Stie had no contact with his maternal grandparents and limited contact with the paternal side.

As a young boy, Stie Fold was generally very fearful, and he had experienced a lot of nightmares. As a result, it was not uncommon that he would end up sleeping in his father's bed. The proximity created a sense of safety and protection. Stie remembers one night he fell asleep in his dad's arms, and when Stie woke up in the morning, his dad was unresponsive when Stie tried to wake him. Stie's father had overdosed and died during the night.

Stie carried a lot of guilt because he felt like he "should have" been able to recognize his father was ill or distressed and called for help. Stie blamed himself for his father's death. On a cognitive level, Stie realized that this was irrational, but on an emotional level, that guilt was engraved into his core belief system. He had come to believe that he would be abandoned by everyone he loved and that he was powerless to do anything about it.

As you can imagine, such a belief system stymied any meaningful connections with the foster families that cared for him. As an adult, he rarely engaged in relationships with partners, and any interactions he had were impersonal and highly sexual. He created barriers to any meaningful connection with others and had a pattern of disappearing both physically and emotionally anytime emotional intimacy began to blossom in his life. Past treatment programs had been unsuccessful; as he started to feel connected to the group (or his therapist), he would move into a flight pattern and would prematurely discharge from the program.

Stie's primary goal for this round of treatment was to resolve his father's death. He even created a grieving ritual. This new goal gave him more motivation to stay in treatment than before, but he still began to slide as he became more connected to me and the group. Then one day in session, he talked about how guilty he felt that he could not remember what his father looked like, I felt impressed to guide him through an imagery.

I invited Stie to do "something weird" and to close his eyes. I told him, "Imagine a group of people that has your best interest at heart. Ask that group of people, Do you love me? And feel the response! Then, invited your Higher Power to step forward from the crowd. This can be God, Allah, Universe, Mother God, or whatever that looks like to you. Ask, Do you love me? And feel the response!"

Once that space was established, I guided him to face his grief using this template. "In your mind, invite the Higher Self of your father to talk with you. Your father is not obligated to participate, but make the invitation and see if he is willing to sit down and talk with you." Although I was prepared to prompt the interaction between Stie and his father, I realized this was unnecessary. Instead of signaling to me that his father was willing, Stie became tearful and twitched in the way that showed he was fully engaged and connected. Instead of interrupting, I sat in silence and just co-experienced the feelings of grief with him. After a period of silent tears, a peaceful smile spread over Stie's face. That serene expression sat for another few minutes before he indicated he was ready.

Stie described later that when invited, his father had burst forward from the group of people and embraced Stie. The sensation in Stie's mind was almost visceral, like he could feel his father's arms around him. As Stie received this warm, loving hug in his mind, conversation between Stie Fold and his father emerged naturally and uninhibited.

Once he indicated he was ready to continue I prompted him, "Now I want to invite the little Stie into the room, to join you and your father. Talk about your experience with your younger self and the impact it had on your development." After some ego state work with the little Stie, we began the closure process. "Invite little Stie to hug your father. Let little Stie tell your father anything that little Stie felt was left unaddressed, and have him listen to what your father had to tell him. When they're done, give little Stie Fold a hug yourself, repeating the same process of exchanging any thoughts or feelings you feel are yet unresolved. Then do the same with your father. When you are finished and ready, open your eyes and return to this space."

Stie Fold was an articulate young man, and he excitedly walked through the conversation and exchange with the father, including launching into the initial embrace and verbal (mental) exchange with his father that had transpired. The format mirrored the instructions that I would typically provide, but it was fun to see the spontaneous creation of that exchange with his father.

Stie later that day told staff that he was going to stay in treatment and that there was so much personal work for him to do that leaving early would get in the way of the healing he needed to maintain sobriety. After his insurance dropped funding at forty-five days, he pulled from his savings to fund an additional fifteen days of treatment. He felt like having cash in the bank was a backdoor plan to relapse, so it was better spent getting healthy than relapsing into his addiction.

Independent of this particular imagery Stie had been engaging his therapeutic process in a positive way. His resistance to relationship and treatment had already begun to shift. I don't believe this one imagery session was the only reason Stie decided to stay in treatment, but I know that the session was part of the equation. Stie more fully engaged in group in real and meaningful ways. He was vulnerable with his peers and began to make emotional connections which he embraced. What a shift from the patterns previously established. It was a thing of beauty.

Gru

This next story has some odd components, and I have not had a session that mirrored these dynamics before or after. It was the first example that came to mind as I was putting together this book, but because it may lack replicability, I did not want to include it as the only example. Yet following my intuition is important to me, and because it has stayed on my mind, I will include the story here as a peculiar experience dealing with grief despite the aforementioned limitations.

The setting for this session was once again during a wilderness trip. Once a year, we would take the boys from the group home on a six-day, five-night, fifty-mile therapeutic wilderness hike through a series of slot canyons in the desert. Towards the end of the hike, the boys were left "solo" for a night. Each boy was provided an alcove in a canyon that was protected from the elements. Each alcove was within a short distance of a staff basecamp but isolated enough that each boy was not within visual contact of each other.

The boys were left from Thursday morning until Friday evening in their "solo spots." They had food and water and a packet of therapy assignments. Staff roamed throughout the day checking on the kids, and the therapists would go out and do therapy sessions. Each of the boys would have a therapy session each day of the solo experience.

Gru was a bit distinct from some of the other clients at the facility because of the pervasive nature of his illegal behaviors. Our facility mostly worked with adolescents with sexual behavior problems; it was less common to have clients with experiences with illegal drugs, violence, or other co-occurring adolescent pathology. Gru was an exception. He had a history of intense substance abuse, albeit isolated to marijuana and hallucinogens, and he had a history of aggressive behavior. He was also a talented skate and snowboarder, showing an athleticism and coordination that many of the kids at the facility lacked. As such he presented as a stark juxtaposition to many of the other boys in the home that were a bit more socially isolated and awkward as a whole.

Gru was fifteen years old when he entered residential treatment. About a year before, he had lost his mother to an aggressive cancer. It had been less than six months between diagnosis and her passing. Before her death, Gru had already started down a path of drug use, absenteeism, poor school performance, and an interest in urban art (graffiti). He had several run-ins with law enforcement in the time leading up to his mom's diagnosis. His father was an introverted individual that had never really talked about the loss of his wife with his son. Their relationship was tenuous at best. Dad resented Gru for exacerbating the stress in the family leading up to and during the illness of his wife, and Gru felt like his father was detached and uncaring both towards him and towards his dying mother.

Dad coped with his grief by training intensively for a series of marathons. Gru coped with his grief with marijuana, hallucinogens, and rebelling generally. After several stints in detention and a growing rap sheet, it was discovered that Gru had sexually abused a younger female cousin. He then came to residential care where I became his therapist.

Gru was bright, articulate, manipulative, and fun to work with. He was very unmotivated to change his substance abuse. He felt like the sexual abuse of his cousin was an anomaly; he felt that he had learned his lesson and did not need to be in treatment with "these kids." He was judgmental towards the other residents, and his relationship with his father was so strained that neither wanted to engage in the weekly family sessions that were offered.

As summer came into fruition, preparations for the therapeutic wilderness adventure were in full bloom. Gru was excited about the idea because he enjoyed the outdoors, and he had heard rumors about some of the fun activities we do. He was looking forward to the adventure. Once on the wilderness trip, Gru quickly emerged as one of the group leaders. He was positive and supportive of his peers and shed much of the condescension that had impeded peer relations prior to the trip.

During his solo experience, he had been very contemplative about the therapeutic assignments he had been given, and he had filled his journal with thoughts and notes over the course of the two days. The session we had together the second day of the solo experience was particularly interesting. It was rare that Gru would talk about his mother, but on this day, she was the first topic he brought up. He mirrored the negative talk of his father as Gru described himself as "killing his mom." He said he knows cancer killed her, but he had not made it easy, and they left on bad terms. He was embarrassed that after she died, he had promised her that he would reform his delinquent behaviors and change his life's trajectory.

This personal commitment he had made to her while she lay in her coffin had only lasted a few days. He had a blow out with his father, left the home, used marijuana, participated in some "urban art," and found himself arrested. After that moment, he jumped into that lifestyle with reckless abandon. He kept himself in a perpetual high and had little to no regard for the rules of his home or society. Gru wept as he talked about how disappointed his mom would have been if she could have seen him now.

As we sat there in the soft sand of the alcove, I asked him, "Do you wanted to try something a little weird?" He closed his eyes and took a few deep breaths. "Imagine a group of people that have your best interest at heart. They could be alive or dead, known or unknown, anyone throughout all humanity, but they must have this one thing in common: your best interest at heart. Let me know when that group has gathered in your mind's eye." Once he indicated, I instructed him, "Ask this group, Do you love me? And then feel the response!"

This process was repeated for his Higher Power. Once this was established, I asked him, "Do you want to invite both your mom and dad in for some family therapy?" Both accepted the invitation. "Invite them to sit in a circle with yourself. Talk to them about your experience over the last few years, and talk them through the loss of your mom and the impact that it has had on you and your relationship with your father."

As Gru began to work through this imagery in his mind's eye, there was an emotional connectedness that was almost palpable. He had never demonstrated much emotion, but as he worked through things in his mind's eye, he had a constant flow of tears down the side of his face. He was not bawling or in the throes of uncontrolled grief, but he was emotionally connected and experiencing the sadness that had been pooling in his angry soul for the last few years.

As we sat there in silence, I repeatedly had the thought that I should give him some space. That seemed like such an odd thought to me; I had never left a client in the throes of an imagery session, and I felt I had the obligation to ensure he was safe and put back together at the close of the session. But that thought or feeling repeatedly imposed itself on me until I consented to the intuitive tug. I told Gru that I felt impressed to give him some space but that I wanted him to continue with his "group therapy" session with his parents until it came to completion. Afterward he could send for me when he was ready.

Grief

At that I got up and left. It was very odd, but felt right. I went on to work with another young man. After finishing that session I returned to Gru to check in. When I walked up to his space he was sitting up silently leaning against the rock face. I asked him if he wanted to check in and he invited me to sit down. He went on to tell me that he had finished his "session" with his parents just moments earlier.

In the wilderness, there is no clock, but it is not uncommon for these sessions to go on for one to two hours. That means in addition to the time I had spent with him (probably thirty to sixty minutes), he had gone on to engage this session in his mind's eye for at least an additional hour. This is the only session I have ever walked away from a client while they were actively engaged in the internal dialogue of imagery, yet in this instance it seemed to be the right choice.

When I returned, Gru described his experience. "I feel a sense of relief that I am loved by both of my parents. I gained some insights to my father's grief; he feels unsure how to help me. I've realized that my father's distance is a method of coping with grief. He's not avoiding me. I've also come to realize that despite any imperfections or difficult behaviors I have, I was not the cause of my mother's death, and she loved me. She told me that I was her little baby, and no matter what happened, she would love me. Her love for me was not contingent on performance." This unfailing love is what Carl Rogers would call "Unconditional Positive Regard." It is love without end.

With this new perspective, Gru gained a piece of mind that he had not previously believed possible. Before he had decided he was simply a bad kid and no treatment, punishment, or intervention would ever positively impact the destructive path he had embarked upon. After engaging in this therapy session in his mind's eye and resolving issues with his mom and dad at this ethereal level, Gru began taking steps to heal the relationship with his father in real life. Gru began to let go of the unhelpful guilt that had driven him into such negative places over the last year.

This became a turning point in the trajectory of his healing. He changed from hopeless to hopeful, from disengaged and detached to engaged and invested.

Conclusion

Therapy is not an event. It is a process. These experiences are not stand-alone healing moments, and there is no immediate "happily ever after" in real life. But there can be a stark shift in a person's motivation to leave the pit of despair in favor of living life and fostering optimism and hope. Losses do not change, but individuals' experiences and relationships with those losses can change.

As I was struggling to prepare to speak at my grandmother's funeral, my wife suggested we do a guided imagery. She was the guide and I was the guided. She brought me through the connection to people that have my best interest at heart and connection to my Divine. In the connection with my grandmother, three distinct stories came to mind, and I knew I needed to share them at the funeral. These became the scaffolding around which I built my address.

The funeral was a very positive experience, and sharing a message of love about my beautiful grandmother was an intensely healing experience. Other family members had memories that were triggered through those stories. This all culminated in a meal after the services where we shared experience and we celebrated the life of this wonderful, faithful women that had given so much of herself for us. At the time she passed away, she had twenty-five grandchildren and twenty-two great grandchildren. Quite the legacy.

The examples here have focused on experiences with death specifically, but this template is not limited to such. I have used it to work through unresolved feelings in relationships after breakups. I do try to shape those interventions so that they are not an imaginary reconciliation but are focused on resolving the unstated so that people can get unstuck and move on. I have used it to address the loss of future expectations. I had a young man whose father was a doctor, and the young man had long had dreams of becoming a physician; but as an adolescent, he had sexually molested several younger family members. With that record, he would never be able to work with vulnerable populations, and the grief imagery was used to reconcile the loss of a long sought-after future that would never be able to materialize. In these cases, I will have them address their Eternal Self for a more cosmic big picture look at things, the goal being to reassure them that despite the loss of one desired future, there are endless possibilities that can result in a positive outcome.

Be creative and listen to intuition. It can be a powerful ally as you navigate the healing space created through imagery work.

Grief Template

- Close your eyes and take a few deep cleansing breaths in sync with me. Then, imagine a group of people that have your best interest at heart. They can be alive or dead, known or unknown, anyone throughout all humanity but they must share this one thing in common, your best interest. When you can see that group of people in your mind's eye, let me know somehow. Grunt, thumbs up, whatever, just let me know they are there.

- Now as you look over that group of people that have your best interest at heart I want you to ask them this questions, Do you love me? And feel the response!

- Now I want you to imagine that from among this group of people that has your best interest at heart steps forward your Higher Power. Vishnu, Buddha, Mother Earth, Christ; whatever that looks like to you. I want you to connect with that being, that essence, and ask the same question, Do you love me? And feel the response.

- I want you to imagine the Eternal Self of your loved one. Not that part of the person that grew old and died [or whatever the circumstance may have been], but that part of him or her that existed before they were born and continues to exist afterwards. Invite that Eternal Self to have a conversation with you. Let me know when he or she is present.

- Take a minute to catch the person up on his or her life. Let them know about how it felt when he or she died and the challenges that came with adjusting to a life without him or her. Talk to the person about your successes and the awesome things that have happened in your life afterward and about the hard times and struggles. Take as long as you need. Let me know when you are done.

- Tell your loved one whatever it is you wished you had time to say before they died [or left], the phrases that have floated around your head and you wished you had only taken the time to say. And then listen to what they wants to tell you. Take as long as you need. Let me know when you're done.

- Now, give your loved one a hug. Let your love for him or her be known. Whisper it into his or her ear and tell the person anything else you feel would be important. Then listen to what he or she has to tell you. Take as long as you want.

- When you are ready, just open your eyes and come back into this space.

MEMORY RECALL

Flawed Memories

Memory is a curious thing. It is an imperfect record of the past, and yet it shapes and colors our perceptions and experiences in the present. Over the years, I have had interest in the dynamics of memory, one of which is eyewitness accounts of events. Eyewitness accounts are often given automatic credit and treated as incontrovertible fact.

Think about this for a moment. If you own a small shop that sells trinkets and one of your employees came up to you and stated, "I think that kid just stole something." The word "think" is not a confident term, so you press the employee a bit. "Why do you think he stole something?" The employee reports that the kid was continually looking around the shop and would touch and pick things up, but instead of inspecting the objects, he would look around the room and then put them back. In addition, the kid was carrying a backpack in hand in a way to intentionally obscure what he was holding.

In this scenario, we have a lot of little indicators that are interesting yet touching and holding objects and looking around would be circumstantial evidence. The collection of observations raises suspicion but is not necessarily incriminating. In such a case, would you confront the kid? Would you pull him aside and asked to look in his bag? Would such actions be appropriate? Would you give him the benefit of the doubt?

Let's play this out in a slightly different way. Imagine that the employee came up to you and said, "That kid just put a candy bar in his backpack. I saw it." Said with those words, is there any doubt about your approach? Would you feel more comfortable confronting the behavior? In the first scenario, there was a lot of suspicious activity; in the second, the facts seemed to lay bare. But is that the case? Could there be alternative explanations?

The Innocence Project is an interesting group that is challenging some of the assumptions made regarding policies and procedures in law enforcement that may contribute to the incarceration of innocent people. The project team identifies eyewitness testimony as the number one factor in the conviction of innocent individuals. In most of these cases, the primary exonerating evidence is DNA testing. In some cases, the project team has been able to corroborate DNA samples with an actual perpetrator of the crime, and there are several situations where the actual perpetrator later confessed to the crime. The Innocence Project suggests that more than 70% of wrongful convictions were in part influenced by eyewitness misidentification (Trainum, 2016).

In an interesting study, Shaw and Porter conducted in 2015 attempted to plant false memories in subjects (Shaw J. P., 2015). They attempted to convince each college-student-aged candidate that he or she had committed a crime or experienced a specific emotional event as an early adolescent (between eleven and fourteen years old). The family of each participant verified that in those years he or she had no history with criminal activity or the police, and that they had not experienced the specific traumatic experience they were planting as a memory, but did have some sort of stressful life event around that time.

The participants were divided into three groups. The first group was told that they had committed a crime, such as theft or assault. The second group was told they had a traumatic experience, such as being attacked by a dog or losing a large amount of money. The third group, the control group, had no memory manipulation.

When interviewed, questions about the false memory would be introduced. Participants were told to recall where they were living at the time and to identify a friend that they spent a lot of time with during that period of their life. After that initial interview, the participants were told to go home and "try to remember more" about the event (false memory); they were also told "most people can remember more if they 'try hard enough.'" Each night after the interview, participants were to think about the event including *context reinstatement*, which is recalling facts around the event such as the participant's age and clothing and the time of day of the event.

Each interviewer used the same script with all participants and tried to portray "incontrovertible" evidence that the event had happened. Each interviewer would use the names of family and contextually relevant friends and made statements such as "your mom told us" or "John Doe remembers when." The goal was to pressure the participant to recall the incident.

In 70% of the crime memory scenarios and 77% of the trauma memory scenarios, the participants endorsed these false memories during later interviews. These participants were intelligent university students, and yet they were psychologically manipulated into believing false memories were real. There are many other studies that reinforce these ideas including how syntax and word selection in questions can influence the recall of a memory (Shaw J. , 2016).

The point is that when working with memory of past events, there is an extra layer of caution that is important for clinicians in their approach and methods. The way we interact, interview, and engage with a client can shape the quality, quantity, type of information that we receive. Generally it is important to use open ended questions, avoid leading questions (questions that have an implied answer, such as, "You put that candy bar in your backpack, didn't you?"), create opportunities for uninterrupted narrative, and not make assumptions (for example, thinking, "I have seen this type of behavior in clients before, and it is always because they were sexually abused").

Intersection of Psychodynamic and CBT

Early therapeutic interventions developed by Freud, Jung, and other great thinkers relied on digging into the past to resolve developmental blocks. The emphasis on the past could at times have the unintended effect of projecting blame onto others outside the individual (parents being a common target, such as in double bind theory). In the mid-1900s, there was a shift from psychoanalysis and issues of subconscious influence to the more empirically driven cognitive behavioral therapy (CBT) framework. Cognitive behavioral therapy became the hegemon of clinical practice (and for the most part remains so to this day).

Unlike early forms of therapy, CBT is hyper focused on the present moment and the fundamentals of behavior. Ultimately the goal of CBT is to track behaviors or thoughts through a cycle of behaviors and consequences that are either desirable or undesirable. Therapists use CBT to help clients shape the thoughts and behaviors that result in undesirable and problematic behaviors (suicidality, criminality, addiction, etc.). In this system, the past is irrelevant; it is viewed as tertiary to the work of developing healthy and appropriate actions leading to prosocial outcomes.

In my personal practice, I see value in both the historical models (Freud and Jung) and the present focus models (CBT). I view these two systems as complementary. I recognize that the goal of therapy is to help clients find healing pathways in the present, and this often involves being more aware of one's thoughts and feelings and how they play out in dysfunctional behavior patterns. But I also believe that attachment templates and trauma play an unconscious role in development. Both of these require attention and intervention.

One way of thinking about this would be if a person was shot. Medical professionals could stop the bleeding, seal up the wound, and apply anti-bacterial ointments or pills to stave off infection. Aesthetically things look good and the person can heal. But if the bullet is left inside their body, at some point, it may create additional complications. In this analogy CBT is like treating the surface wound and the

Freudian type interventions would be like pulling out the bullet.

"Do no harm" is a therapeutic maxim that is worth remembering as I discuss this next template/intervention. These cautions are not to scare off someone from using the template, but they are to inform and educate readers on the ethical issues that exist around exploring memory. This template should only be used if it is something that they client initiates or if it has clear therapeutic application. I would caution against using imagery work to extract repressed memories that a clinician assumes is present when lacking any evidence to the contrary. Not all pathological behaviors in the present are connected to pathological experiences of the past.

Memory Recall Template

In the even it would be appropriate to explore memory using imagery work with a client it would be set up in the same manner all previous imageries were done. I might say something like: "Do you want to try something a little weird?

"Close your eyes. Imagine a group of people that have your best interest at heart. They can be alive or dead, known or unknown, anyone throughout all humanity, but they must have your best interest at heart. When you can see this group in your minds eye I want you to ask them, Do you love me? And feel the response!" Typically, I give this a minute and let them experience the feelings before I continue.

"Now I want you to imagine that from among this group with your best interest at heart steps forward you Higher Power. The Universe, Mother God, Vishnu, Christ, whatever that might look like to you. Ask your Higher Power that same question, Do you love me? And feel the response!" Pause.

Memory

Once the foundations are laid, I will typically use something very similar to the trauma template where I have them select 2 individuals to help them through the experience. "As you look out over this group of people that have your best interest at heart, I want you to ask for two volunteers. Two people that can accompany you and your Higher Power on a journey of sorts." Once they have identified these people I ask if they want to share the names. If they chose to do so I will use the names throughout the imagery, otherwise I just generically reference the dream team as I continue through the template.

"Once you have identified your dream team I want you to imagine an experience that shuffles from light to dark, like going through a tunnel with periodic windows. I want you to imagine a vehicle to travel through this tunnel. Once you have this in your minds eye I want you to imagine inviting your dream team to travel with you. You get into the vehicle together, and then ask your Higher Power to take you back in time. Ask for him to take you to a time in your life that has left a gap in your mind, a void where you cannot remember." Once these foundations are set then you want to ensure that they have an emotional safety net, so they do not become overwhelmed by an experience. I might say something like: "Before we go further I just want to remind you that we have a lot of magical powers that come from being in our mind. We can pause things, rewind, fast-forward, make things big or small, or black and white. This is important because as we remember things if something is overwhelming we can pause and take a break, modify it so it is easier to work with.

"With that in mind I want you to ask your Higher Power to take you through the tunnel. The tunnel will alternate from light to dark as you travel. In the dark moments it represents the passage of time. In the light moments you will see into experiences in your past, in dark moments time will flow by. I want you to ask to stop if you get to a memory that you would like to explore, or something that you had forgotten. You can ask to spend more time in that spot. When you are ready feel free to proceed." At this point I sit in silence as the client goes through the experience. Some will explain things they see, some will not. But often I will prompt them saying, "When you come to a memory of interest let me know, and if it is helpful you can tell me what you see, or just let me know when you have seen what you need to and let me know you are moving on." It can be helpful if you are moving through multiple memories to at least know when things shift from one theme to another, even if no explanation is provided.

You may have noted that this template is almost identical to the one for the trauma imagery. Basically I use the same dynamics, but with a slightly different purpose. In this case we are looking for understanding and context, in trauma imagery we are looking to re-story traumatic experiences of the past. There are times that a memory exercise will naturally evolve into a trauma resolution intervention. Nevertheless, as stated previously, it is worth being cautious with such explorations because although memory imagery can create understanding, there is also risk of false memories and not all things that are experienced in imagery are a direct reflection of real experiences. It is more about making meaning and creating context to experiences in life, than about creating a perfect recreation of the past. Memory just does not work that way.

Waz Up

Dr. Weaver, my mentor, was trained in hypnosis, as were most of the early psychologists. I was working with a client who had sexually abused two young neighbor boys while he was babysitting them. If I had this case to do over again, I may not have approached it in the way I did at that time, but that was many years ago and my opinions have changed. I will just use this as one illustration. Waz Up was adopted right from the hospital room of the biological mother. For all intents and purposes, it was an ideal situation for an adoption, maximizing the probability of strong attachment and bond with the adoptive parents.

Unfortunately, this young man was emotionally aloof and poorly attached in general. Waz was socially aware and showed strong perspective-taking abilities but struggled with empathy and respecting rules and boundaries throughout childhood and early adolescents. His adoptive parents were loving and engaged (overly engaged in some ways) and they were caught up in the abused-abuser cycle myth, assuming he had been sexually abused when he was younger. This had become their favorite explanation for his sexually exploitive behaviors, and they continually pressured him to 'remember.'

I did not know much about memory work and turned to my mentor, Dr. Weaver. I requested that he do some hypnosis to explore the issue. He readily consented to the idea and came to our session the next week. This was with the consent of the client who worked with Gary in group therapy and had a pre-established relationship. I sat back to watch what I assumed would be my first observation of clinical hypnosis, but what happened instead was the familiar imagery work that I had studied with Gary for some time.

Gary asked Waz Up, "Imagine a group of people that has your best interest at heart. When you have this group in your mind, ask them, Do you love me? And then take a moment to feel the response." Gary also had Waz connect with his Higher Power in the standard way. Then Gary said, "I want you to ask your Higher Power to take you back to a time when you were sexually abused." Obviously, you could use any incident or focus for imagery, but in this case, Gary was looking to uncover sexual victimization.

In this case, nothing came up. It was dark, and no memories came to mind. Gary did not push Waz and concluded that either he had not been abused or was not capable of remember it. Either way, the therapeutic goal for this young man was to work with the present problems, and I advised his parents that further digging into the past was contraindicated. They were asked to put this pet theory aside so we could move forward in therapy.

Given some of the research on false memories that I am now familiar with, I would have been more reticent to have attempted an imagery to recall an unknown traumatic event at the parents bidding. In this case example, there was plenty of space to reinforce the concept of inventing a past story or confabulating one and opening the door to a false confession.

Polygraph

I am aware of the ongoing and evolving controversy around polygraph. Most therapists have never used this tool as part of their practice. Polygraph use seems to be isolated to fidelity marriage counselling and sex offender therapy. Therapists use it with people who sexually offend to ensure a full disclosure of all abusive behaviors and to ensure safety in current behaviors. Full disclosure of all victims can open up the possibility to offer recovery services to victims and abusive cycles can be interrupted.

Although only a small proportion of clinicians use this intervention, I hope that the example is not so foreign that it lacks applicability in other contexts. Most of my career has been focused on adolescents that have sexually harmed others, so I will use my experience working with boys who have been polygraphed as the most common pragmatic implementation of this particular imagery.

I have never collected precise statistics on my clients' experiences with polygraph, but I would guess about 70% of them will pass their first sex-history polygraph, validating they have disclosed all the victims. A significant portion of those that pass the polygraph make additional disclosures during the exam; either about additional victims or additional details regarding their offense. This added information through the polygraph aids in treatment planning and addressing safety issues for families and the community. I have had great success working with this population over the years, and I always felt like fostering rapport with clients was one of my strengths. Yet when it comes to talking about this intensely shameful behavior with potential legal and familial consequences, rapport is not always sufficient to fostering honest disclosure. In addition, I worked in a system that had a policy of using polygraph on all appropriate clients. In other words, I have facilitated this intervention with many, many clients over the years.

I will not use a specific case example in this scenario, but I will describe a collective experience with clients that fail the polygraph and continue to deny any memory of additional victims. When this scenario plays out in my office, I will first use the tactic of unifying myself with the client against the "polygraph"—I basically personify the instrument, usually referring to it as "the box."

When I have a client return from a failed polygraph, the first thing I do in session is ask them, "What do you think happened? Why are you failing this test?" In some cases, the client will talk about additional sexual contacts that they failed to disclose. Usually these are family members, same-sex encounters, or animals—memories that sometimes triggers shame and discomfort and are difficult to talk about; which is understandable, any of us would be reticent to talk about the intimate details of our sexual lives with others.

Those who continue to deny any additional sexual contacts will sometimes say things like, "Maybe it happened and I can't remember." I invite disclosure but do not bear down on the client. In our program, clients did not lose privileges or receive specific consequences for failing a polygraph, but they were "stuck" on that specific phase in their treatment until we could work through and resolve the issue. Typically, I would work with the client for a few weeks, and in the event that they had no additional disclosures, I would say something like, "Well, you know, at some point we are going back to face 'the box.' I really want you to do well, and I know that you want to be honest about things. So what are we going to do to help you be successful? What do you think ought to happen so that next time we have a different outcome than what you experienced your first time?"

My goal here is to align myself with the client and to externalize the problem. The problem is "the box" or the failed polygraph. The solution then is honesty or, in this case, "aided memory." It is very common that the boys will ask me if I know anything that could help them remember if something really did happen that they just couldn't remember. With that invitation, I would often walk into memory imagery work. When they ask, they have petitioned for help. They want to be honest and open, and to "beat" the polygraph. They want to remember.

Then I set it up as follows: "Imagine a group of people that has your best interest at heart. Alive or dead, known or unknown, anyone throughout all eternity but they must have this one common thread, your best interest at heart. Let me know when you can see them and give me a grunt or thumbs up or something." Pause. "Now ask that group of people that has your best interest at heart, Do you love me? And feel the response." Pause. "As you are looking over this group of people that have your best interest at heart, imagine that your Higher Power steps forward. Allah, Mother Earth, Buddha, Christ, whatever that looks like to you. Connect with that Being, that essence, that power, and ask the same question, Do you love me? And feel the response!"

"Now, as we get ready for this experience, I want you to imagine a place in your mind's eye that alternates between dark and light or fast and slow. It can be anything, but try to think of something that would fit that description that rotates between contrasts. When you have that image in your mind, tell me about it." The client then describes whatever image comes to them. In this case, let's say there is a ride at the local them park with a pirate ship that sways back and forth, and at the peak, it is like time stops for a second before the ship quickly swings to the other side then stalls out at the top of the pendulum.

Armed with that imagery, I invite the client, "Imagine being on the ride at night. Imagine the sounds of the different rides and all the rolling lights of the theme park, and maybe the rumble of voices and life going on around you. But, when you get on the pirate ship for this ride, there are only two passengers: you and your Higher Power. And, this time, as the ship reaches the pinochle of the pendulum, a little hologram pops open and has a scene from your life that plays. In those moments, pause at the peak of the ride until you are ready to move on."

If this was the ichnography the client was drawing from, I would probably add things like, "I want you to get on and set up your lap support. You know that bar you have to press down and it locks into place until the ride is over. When you have your support on tight, I want you to double check your Higher Power. Did he put his on? If not you tell him he has to and make sure that he is secure. We don't want to lose anybody. When you are ready, there is the little teenager with acne that looks like he hates every moment of his job, and he comes over the intercom droning on about keeping your hands and arms inside the ride at all times. You know that whole spiel."

"Now I want you to turn to your Higher Power and ask him to take you back in time, back to the first thing that you might need to remember, so that you can do well on your polygraph exam. Tell him that you really want to be honest and pass the test, but you are worried there is something that you can't remember. Ask him if he can help take you back there."

"Then the ride begins. You start to slowly work your way up. At first, you don't get that high, but eventually you get that knotted feeling in your stomach as the g-forces drive you down through the swing of the pendulum, and when you reach the top, an image appears. The image is a hologram of a past experience in your life. The more you swing the further back you go into your life. You will continue to see images of yourself getting younger and younger."

"Eventually the ride will pause, and a memory will be in front of you. When things are paused and you have a memory sitting in front of you, which memory will be important to know for you to do well on your polygraph, tell me what you see."

Throughout past templates, I have told you to just allow your client to have his or her experience without trying to voyeur on the process. This template is one of the exceptions. In this case, I want my client to talk, and I am going to take notes. So, when the client is looking at the memory, he or she will begin to describe the scene. Often the first scene a client will describe is a memory he or she has already disclosed—not always, but such is not uncommon. Once the client reaches the end of the narrative, I say, "Now turn to your Higher Power and ask him, What's next? And the ride will continue to sway through the pendulums projecting images of your life until there is something that is important that you remember. When you get to that point let me know; take as much time as you like."

Within a short period of time, the client will signal, and I have them describe what he or she is seeing. And we repeat this process over and over. At the end of each disclosure, I simply tell my client to turn to his or her Higher Power and ask for the next scene. Eventually the client will exhaust all the scenarios and will say something like, "There is nothing else." When that happens, I move to close. In this scenario, the client would imagine the ride slowing the swinging motion and eventually coming to a halt. The lap belts would release and he or she would shuffle off the ride. I would then tell the client, "Find a private place where it was just you and your Higher Power. When you find a place, embrace one another. Thank your Higher Power and tell him anything that you feel like you need to say, and then listen to what you Higher Power says back. And then, when you are ready, open your eyes and come back into this space."

Conclusion

It never ceases to surprise me how often this little exercise will provide additional disclosures, and often *many* additional disclosures of illegal sexual behavior. I debate with myself often in these scenarios if the boy is actually "remembering" something or if the situation is just non-threatening enough that it invites the disclosure. I honestly don't know if it is one or the other, but I can say that it has been highly effective. In place of a client feeling beaten down and violated in order to get a more full disclosure, he or she often speaks in terms like "a weight has been lifted" or "feeling lighter."

I believe there is something powerfully healing about shedding our secrets. I think there is a reason in twelve-step programs two of the steps are to make a searching and fearless moral inventory and admit to God, self, and another person the exact nature of wrongdoings (N/A, 1939). "Owning our story can be hard but not nearly as difficult as spending our lives running from it. Embracing our vulnerabilities is risky but not nearly as dangerous as giving up on love and belonging and joy—the experiences that make us the most vulnerable. Only when we are brave enough to explore the darkness will we discover the infinite power of our light." This quote comes from *The Gifts of Imperfection* by Brene Brown, an expert shame researcher and author of some powerful books on courage and connection (Brown, 2010).

There are times when a client is seeking help to explore memories he or she is unable to retrieve. I believe guided imagery is a tool we should be careful with, but I also believe it has its place in the tool kit.

Memory Recall Template

- Close your eyes. Imagine a group of people that have your best interest at heart. They can be alive or dead, known or unknown, anyone throughout all humanity, but they must have your best interest at heart. When you can see this group in your minds eye, I want you to ask them, Do you love me? And feel the response!

- Now I want you to imagine that from among this group with your best interest at heart steps forward you Higher Power. The Universe, Mother God, Vishnu, Christ, whatever that might look like to you. Ask your Higher Power that same question, Do you love me? And feel the response!

- As you look out over the group of people that have your best interest at heart, I want you to ask for two volunteers. Two people that can accompany you and your Higher Power on a journey of sorts.

- Once you have identified your dream team I want you to imagine an experience that shuffles from light to dark, like going through a tunnel with periodic windows. I want you to imagine a vehicle to travel through this tunnel. Once you have this in your minds eye I want you to imagine inviting your dream team to travel with you. You get into the vehicle together, and then ask your Higher Power to take you back in time. Ask for him to take you to a time in your life that has left a gap in your mind, a void where you cannot remember.

- Before we go further I just want to remind you that we have a lot of magical powers that come from being in our mind. We can pause things, rewind, fast-forward, make things big or small, or black and white. This is important because as we remember things if something is overwhelming we can pause and take a break, modify it so it is easier to work with.

- With that in mind I want you to ask your Higher Power to take you through the tunnel. The tunnel will alternate from light to dark as you travel. In the dark moments it represents the passage of time. In the light moments you will see into experiences in your past, in dark moments time will flow by. I want you to ask to stop if you get to a memory that you would like to explore, or something that you had forgotten. You can ask to spend more time in that spot. When you are ready feel free to proceed.
- When you come to a memory of interest let me know, and you if it is helpful you can tell me what you see, or just let me know when you have seen what you need to and let me know you are moving on.
- Repeat the above until they do not have anything more; and then invite them to open their eyes and come back into this space.

RANDOM TIDBITS

Eclectic Collection

The following stories are just a few examples of scenarios where guided imagery was used but the cases did not fit squarely into one of the templates. Two purposes in providing these examples are to 1) demonstrate the flexibility of guided imagery and 2) provide a few additional examples of ways it has been successfully applied in clinical situations.

DITHL

Have you ever driven at night and found that you were approaching a deer? The deer is in the middle of the road and is staring directly at you as you come flying down the road in its direction, but the deer does not do anything but watch you approach. It can be quite frustrating because you would think survival instincts would kick in and send the deer fleeing in any other direction. But sometimes it just stands their wide eyed. In a worst case scenario, you could hit the animal damaging property and putting the safety of the animal and passengers at risk.

Once in a while, when a boy first arrives at the facility, he has that dear in the head lights (DITHL) look. My heart goes out to these boys because shifting from living in their home to living with a bunch of strangers must be seriously difficult. Add to that the strict schedule and regimen of residential treatment, and it is a wonder that more clients don't arrive with that look in their eyes.

One of these was a boy of 13 years old. He and his parents came in and met with the residential director, took a tour of the facility and were introduced to the other boys, and had a therapy session with me. After I had gathered some background information and some ideas for goals, the family left the boy and the facility.

In this case, the boy, whom we will call DITHL, looked so very nervous it seemed he was holding back tears. After some preliminary probes to get to know him and gather some information, it was clear to me that he was stuck. He was struggling to focus, answer questions, and engage. When the usual rapport-building seemed to be stifled, I ran the boy through a simple imagery.

I simply told him, "I know you are scared, and this entire situation is probably very overwhelming. Would you mind if we did something a bit weird?" The boy nodded assent, and without any further explanation, I simply told him to close his eyes. We took a few deep cleansing breaths together, and then I said, "Imagine a group of people who have your best interest at heart. They can be alive or dead, known or unknown, anyone throughout all humanity, but they must have this one thing in common: your best interest. When you can see that group of people in your mind's eye or you feel them present let me know." Pause. "Ask that group of people, Do you love me? And feel the response!"

After a short pause, I directed, "Imagine your Higher Power. God, Buddha, Shiva, or whatever that looks like to you. Connect with that power, with that being, with that entity. Then ask it the same question: Do you love me? And feel the response."

I let that sink in for a minute. Then I simply told him to open his eyes when he was ready. In that brief intervention, DITHL had gone from looking tearful and overwhelmed to relaxed and present. I shifted gears back into gathering his background and goals for treatment. He was much calmer and more engaged as we moved forward in the conversation, and what started out as an unproductive and tense interaction evolved into a connected and rapport-building interaction.

To be clear, this is not something I would do with every client. In fact, I rarely use this in the first interventions with a client. But in this situation, there was that intuitive tug where this method just felt right. Acting on the feeling provided a foundation of hope for an overwhelmed young man that was lost in his own amygdale's response to placement in residential care. Instead of a passive, question-response exchange that would not have fostered any feelings of safety, DITHL was able to connect and feel cared for in his first therapeutic exchange.

Jolly Pop

When a client is coming off of drugs, he or she experiences a withdrawal period that can be very difficult physiologically. It is important to have medical oversight in many of these situations both to ensure the safety of the client as well as to maximize the likelihood he or she will continue treatment. It is not uncommon that medications are used as a short-term transition (few days up to a week) from the toxic levels the client is at when he or she arrives in treatment to a more functioning state.

The folk wisdom in the field indicates that after the initial detox, it takes about a month to "get your body back" and two months to "get you mind back." Obviously periods of detox varies based on the type of drug, quantity of use, period of time one has been using, and so on. But it is not uncommon that in those first days of detox, the client is completely physically and emotionally wiped out. All programs have different approaches and expectations for the detox period, but our program typically gives the client 24–48 hours to detox before he or she is expected to follow the daily routine and rituals of the center, including participating in gym, groups, house care, and so on. Even once that initial detox has cleared from a client's system, there are at times a psychological craving for his or her drug of choice.

One day I was in my therapy office when a young lady we will call Jolly Pop came to talk about her personal struggles and cravings. She sat down and was visibly shaking and short of breath and generally looked sickly. Jolly wanted to leave and claimed she was just wasting her time in treatment. She had been in the facility for about two weeks, and she described intense cravings and that she could taste her drug of choice in her mouth. She decided she was just not going to be in the position to continue treatment any longer. She needed to leave, and she needed to leave right then. Jolly did not want to discuss alternatives, but because she also did not want to leave disrespectfully (AWOL), she was informing me of her decision.

After some discussion about her plan and what would happen next, it was clear she was more ambivalent about leaving than her initial speech had indicated. She had many concerns, and although she wanted to use, part of her also wanted to get out of this life that had brought her so much pain. Jolly was nervous that the lifestyle was going to kill her, and she knew that if she continued this lifestyle, she likely would lose custody and contact with her child permanently.

I asked, "Would you be willing to try something?" Once she agreed I continued, "Close your eyes and imagine a group of people that have your best interest at heart. They can be alive or dead, known or unknown, anyone throughout all humanity, but they must have this one thing in common: your best interest at heart. Once this group of people are gathered in your mind's eye, I want you to ask them, Do you love me? And feel the response." Pause. "Imagine that from among this group of people that has your best interest at heart steps forward your Higher Power. God, Vishnu, Mother Nature, whatever that looks like to you, and ask the same question: Do you love me? And feel the response."

Once this was established, I said, "I now want you to connect with your Eternal Self, that part of yourself that existed before this life and will exist after—not a future self of goodness that you would want to become, but that part of yourself that is good, powerful, and beautiful even though you are not always able to see or acknowledge it. Talk with your Eternal Self about your cravings and desire to leave the program." After some time, she indicated the conversation had closed. "Ask your Eternal Self for three things you could do to get through the next twenty-four hours successfully."

After receiving some direction from her Eternal Self, we closed the session with her giving the Eternal Self a hug, telling her anything Jolly felt like she needed to say, and listening to anything else her Eternal Self would want her to know.

I can't remember the specific steps Jolly was given to make it through the next twenty-four hours, but I do remember her physiology had drastically changed. When she first came into the office, she was in tears and was trembling all over, and when she held out her hands, there was a significant and unmistakable tremor. When the imagery was over, she was calm and had her body back.

She was shocked at how quickly the overwhelming need to use had been eradicated. She felt fully committed to making the next twenty-four hours work before making any decisions. By the next day, she was stable and safe. She continued her treatment for another forty-five days after that and then transitioned to a long-term (one to two-year program) program that specialized in reuniting families. Jolly Pop had gone from never completing a program (with five previous attempts) to successfully completing residential care with a rigorous transition plan that would require years of commitment, and she joyfully accepted the challenge with a vision of a healthy future and the potential of reuniting with her baby.

There were many things that went into that success story that were not related to this one imagery session, but that session did allow her to be in the program long enough for some of the other pieces to settle and stick. Guided imagery is not "the tool" but "a tool" that is good to have in one's bag of tricks.

Theo Ug

Every once in a while in residential care, there is a youth that needs placement that does not quite fit the mold but has no better alternatives. This story is about one of those scenarios and involves a young man that had some very significant cognitive limitations. He did not reflect our typical client, and he came with unusual challenges.

We are going to call this young man Theo Ug. Thug was one of the young man's favorite words and was how he referred to basically everyone, including himself. We will use the term here with the hope it is not offensive; it is not meant to be derisive. This young man was raised in a tough neighborhood where there were many gangs, drugs, and violence. He had significantly compromised cognitive capacity (IQ 56), which was in part why he was a peculiar placement for our facility.

The issue driving placement was that he had a history of abusive sexual behaviors, and there were no programs that specialized in both his cognitive needs and sexual misbehavior, and the system determined that the priority for placement was the latter; this was to protect his cognitive compromised peers who would be quite vulnerable if Theo's sexual misbehavior was not first addressed. In our program, we had special education teachers on staff, but Theo's needs were high enough that our resources and expertise were strained.

After a few weeks, a routine had developed between Theo and the staff, teachers, and clinicians. He was fairly vulgar in speech. but it was determined this was not an area the program would battle with him unless it was directed at someone and done in a menacing/threatening way. A behavioral modification system was developed where hour to hour privileges and consequences were immediate and fairly brief. If he reacted to receiving a consequence there were no additional consequences piled on him as it was determined this would create an unhealthy cycle with escalating consequences without giving space for Theo Ug to react and recover.

With such accommodations in place a few months passed by in a way that felt fairly successful. Not perfect, but manageable. In residential care, clients often manifest new issues once they become accustomed to the residential routine. For Theo, settling into residential care drew out unresolved post-traumatic stress disorder (PTSD). It started with a nightmare where he remembered being physically assaulted by his father. These dreams turned into daytime flashbacks.

For many people, flashbacks are an internal experience. For Theo Ug, they were an external manifestation. He would cuss and swear at his biological father as if he were present. There were times Theo would throw a punch or push the air as if he were fending off his father in that moment. This behavior was triggered by the nightmares and escalated over a few days to a point that he was becoming unsafe. Staff and teachers worried that he would hurt someone during one of his flashbacks, and his vulgar outbursts were disrupting school and frightening and triggering some of the other kids.

During a staff treatment meeting, this problem was being discussed, and Theo's therapist suggested that he be hospitalized. The delusional component of Theo's PTSD certainly merited this conversation. After some discussion, we decided to proceed with a two-prong approach. My responsibility was to contact and prepare placement for Theo in the hospital. Theo's therapist was to attempt trauma work using guided imagery with Theo that day; if his behavior was a trauma response, then directly treating it with trauma work could mitigate the symptoms.

The therapist later reported a very interesting experience with Theo. During the trauma imagery session with

Theo, he did not sit with his eyes closed as imagery is often done; as the therapist articulated the steps, Theo had his eyes open and acted out the steps of the imagery as if there were people present. Theo connected with the people with his best interest at heart and with his Higher Power, and from that crowd, Theo selected two people to help and support him through the imagery.

When Theo was told to create a plan with his "dream team," the entire plan was talked out actively as he looked at the people in his image as if they were actually present. They put together the plan and were then invited to revisit the traumatic memory and enact the plan. Theo Ug mimed his plan there in the office. He held his father and removed him from the room and then coddled and cared for his younger self. When recounting this, Theo's therapist indicated the session was a bit disorienting to have both the client's eyes open and the physical-spatial activity. But that was the way Theo's brain worked, and it was what he needed. After this trauma imagery session, Theo never again had a flashback as a resident.

Not all interventions are going to be this dramatic, quick, and decisive, but in this case, guided imagery made all the difference and prevented a costly hospitalization. Theo was able to stay in residential treatment and work through some important trauma issues. It is likely the very fact that he felt safe allowed the psychological trigger to work through these issues at that time. It may have stifled the opportunity to do the work if placement had been disrupted. This case illustrates the importance of having options for dealing with troublesome behaviors at the root level.

Lu Ostte

When working with adolescents who have sexually harmed others, they will commonly participate in a reunification process.   Part of this process is writing a *clarification letter*. The clarification letter was really born from the wishes of victims of sexual crimes. It is very common that victims are plagued with self-deprecating guilt by misappropriating accountability onto themselves. Certainly this plight of victims is exacerbated by persistent rape myths, such as dressing a certain way or being in the wrong place at the wrong time invites sexual violence. Clarification letters are a way to rightly transfer a victim's guilt to the perpetrator. These projections of blame onto the victim are wholly inappropriate. Those that perpetrate sexual violence are not unbridled animals that cannot control themselves. They are sentient beings that need to be held accountable for their poor decisions.

When working with adolescents who have perpetrated sexual violence, there are times when they must take accountability for their actions. One way to help them do this is to have them prepare a letter that takes accountability for their actions. The following is an example of the instructions I would provide to therapists new to this method:

The following are some general guidelines for working through clarification letters. This is not comprehensive, and therefor there are inevitably many other themes that could be addressed or ways to go about it. I have found these guidelines to be a support for thinking about clarification letters and how to prepare my clients. I would never just give this list to a client in an attempt to prepare them to write clarification, nor would I coach him or her on exactly what to write or how to say what he or she needs to say. I want the raw product of the client's own mind to have a better idea about the way he or she is thinking about clarification and what his or her natural impulse would be in addressing his or her abusive behaviors with the victim. By seeing what the client puts together without direction, I have the best glimpse into their psyche and where they are at therapeutically. If the clarification is superficial, power-based, or a victim stance, I have great therapeutic material to work with—and it would contraindicated moving into clarification sessions in the near future if they are unable to be accountable. On the other hand, if the client executes a clarification letter well without much guidance, it speaks well of his or her mental and emotional state and therapeutic readiness.

In a clarification letter, ensure the client
- includes a statement that the incident was not the victim's fault.
- the client should take accountability for a specific behavior; this lets the victim know that there has been a full disclosure of all specific behaviors or details.
- provides a *menu of options* of ways the victim may have been impacted.
- does not focus only on the sexual offence but includes any of the other dynamics that were negative in the relationship.
- includes a clear statement about what lead up to the offence (isolation, games, wrestling, positioning for viewing), how the offence took place, and how the offender covered-up or perpetuated the secret (threats, promises, fear statements, lies when confronted, etc.).
- clarifies what has changed so nothing like the abuse will happen again.

- writes the letter appropriate to the age of victim and is language sensitive.

Make sure to eliminate any

- apologies. It may sound weird, but an apology has an expectation of forgiveness and introduces a power dynamic we want to eliminate; clarification done well feels better than an apology with expectation of forgiveness.
- therapeutic jargon or rambling.
- advice to the victim on what he or she should think or feels.
- power dynamics, including the client dictating what the victim should do in the future, protective statements, or anything that has an "I made you _____" component to it.
- "shoulding" statements, which statements are often powerless and not helpful; in the event that it is appropriate, there should be a clear statement about what the alternative expectation would be.
- focus on the offender; the purpose of a clarification is to meet the needs of the victim, not to assuage the guilt of the client that perpetrated the offense.

I used this method with a young man we will call Lu Ostte. He had a low-average intelligence, was fairly young (fourteen years old), and had offended his younger sister. The plan was to engage reunification if both he and his sister were ready. After roughly six months in residential treatment Lu Ostte's parents had indicated that the sister was interested in having contacted with Lu. Lu seemed to be in a stable positive place in treatment so I started coordinating with the therapist the younger sister (victim). Her therapist indicated that it was a good time to move into reunification activities, and therefore I invited Lu to complete a clarification letter.

When completing a formal assignment such as this in the program, clients would be give some basic instructions, but these instruction were intentionally vague and non-specific. For example, a client would be told that I had spoken with the victim's therapist, and we have discussed doing a conjoint session. In preparation for that, the client was to write a letter of clarification and take responsibility for his or her abusive and problematic behaviors. That is about all the instruction the client is given. Certainly none of the specifics listed above are provided (that list was for therapists as they reviewed assignments to look for those dynamics). Typically, the client is given a timeframe for completing the letter, a few weeks being the most common.

When the letter is completed, the client brings it to group for review. The group then provides feedback as to strengths and weaknesses, and the client later revises the letter. This typically will go through two to three iterations. If the client did a great job right from the start, he or she may have it 'passed off' the first round. Similarly, a letter in perpetual revision may indicate that the client has some fundamental thinking errors.

Unfortunately, Lu Ostte was one of these boys that just did not seem to get it. We talked about the issues with his clarification letter repeatedly, but the letter did not improve. He applied some of the ideas, and his letter was not bad in terms of content, but it felt like an English assignment to me, not a heartfelt accountability letter, not something that could provide healing for his sister.

He was frustrated and feeling stuck, and I was concerned that he just lacked the empathic capacity to really see the fundamental purpose of the assignment. These projects are much more than just checking a box but about rebuilding the esteem and wellbeing of the victim that the client potentially compromised with his or her abusive acts.

As we were sitting in session one day, and he moved into a "victim stance" place; he thought it unfairness that the group and I did not recognizing his hard work. I decided to shift gears and jump into an imagery. I said, "Lu, can we do something a bit weird? Imagine a group of people that have your best interest at heart, they can be alive or dead known or unknown. Ask this group, do you love me? And feel the response!

"Imagine your Higher Power and ask, Do you love me? And feel the response!" Once this was established I told him to "Imagine the Eternal Self of your sister, that part of her that existed before she was born and will continue to exist after she dies. Ask her if she would be willing to have a conversation with you?

She consented to the meeting, and they sat down in a room with two chairs where she would feel particularly safe. The iconography for the room was not pulled from his "safe place" but a hypothetical safe place from her perspective. This was to mirror the deferential power dynamic that should exist in a clarification session in real life. They are typically done in the therapy office of the victim or a safe place of the victim's choosing (private or public).

Then he was instructed to, "Ask her what impact your abusive behaviors had on her. I want you to listen to what she says. Let me know when you are done." We then sat in silence for a time. After he said they were done I told him, "please list off some of the things she told you, what specific ways was she impacted by the abuse?" Then we continued, "ask your sister's Eternal Self what she thinks she needs from you so that she can better mover forward at this point in her life?" After he told me he was ready I said, "Rattle off some examples of what she might need to hear from you so she can move on at this point in her life." He was able to list some very profound and important points. As he articulated these points I noted them on a piece of paper.

After this he was told "Imagine asking your sister if she had anything else that she needed from you. Ask her Eternal Self if she would let you give her a hug. If she allows it just wrap her up in a hug and tell her thank you. When you are ready feel free to open your eyes."

In that brief intervention, Lu Ostte shifted from a pragmatic, rote, emotionally detached approach to his clarification to the exact opposite. He was emotionally connected, was focused on his victim's needs from her perspective, and had great insight to what she might need from him so that she could heal and move forward in her treatment.

The letter was completed shortly thereafter, but more importantly, an empathic-emotional shift had taken place in Lu Ostte that laid the foundation for a successful reunification process. It was not just a momentary cognitive shift that allowed him to check a box in treatment, but a relationship-building paradigm shift that opened his eyes to the impact of his abusive behaviors on his sister and what she might need from him for her healing. His focused shifted from lamenting (victim stance) the hardnosed therapist and group to learning to be accountable and focused on others—an important step in his own healing process.

Conclusion

The possibilities for implementing guided imagery are endless. The important feature is to have the confidence to walk into difficult and dark places in a client's treatment process by simply getting out of the way and letting forces greater than yourself do the healing. It is liberating in many ways to not have to be in charge of the change process. The client has internal resources and spiritual assistance that is literally waiting to be unleashed. And imagery is one way of tapping into that resource.

GURU CASE STUDIES

Supervision

I remember after my initial exposure to guided imagery through the wilderness hike with Dr. Gary Weaver I had a strong desire to know what it was he was doing with the kids. It took me a few months to approach him and ask. He was elated to have the opportunity to share. For several years we met for weekly supervision involving imagery work. Recently I came across some old note books and included in those were a few sessions that Gary had done with clients while I observed. Among my notes I had found a few sessions Gary had done on clients where I had attempted to capture the exchange verbatim. My notes were not comprehensive both because I could not write that fast, and at times I was caught up in the experience and failed to write out each word. But the following scenarios come from my supervision journal with Gary with visualizations he had done with the boys.

Stewart Umped

I want to introduce you to a boy we are going to call Stewart (Stu) Umped. He was an energetic and impulsive young man that defaulted to anger anytime that he felt confused, sad, misunderstood, or pretty much anything other than entertained. He had years of therapy, including residential care, prior to coming to the current placement. He had been living in the group home for the better part of six months, and there was fairly limited progress in his overall healing and ability to manage his mood issues. He seemed to be stumped—as did all those trying to help him be his best self.

Stu Umped had a fairly decent awareness of his problems, and he could talk behavioral-thought cycles and copings and articulate a clear plan for success. The problem was that this awareness did not seem to translate into a change of behavior and engagement. Stu had an intense trauma history in his early life, and this provided some understanding for where the dysfunction came from. Unfortunately, he would often place all blame on his past for any blow up, blow out, or melt down that ever occurred.

After some time of feeling stuck with Stu, I had invited Gary to participate in a session with Stu in hopes to find traction towards change. Stu Umped had an ongoing relationship with Gary, so his presence was not introducing a foreign element, but it would provide a new factor to help Stu look at things differently.

Close your eyes. This is kind of like hypnosis. Imagine all the people who have your best interest at heart.

Can you see them?" Gary allows a space for silence. "Ask them, Do you love me?" He again gave a space for silence. "Usually you feel it first at the base of your heart. Let it grow and grow up into your head, through your arms and fingers, and down your legs until it oozes from your toes. Sometimes there is this grey stuff that gets in the way. Melt it away with the powerful feeling of love. Just enjoy this feeling.

"Are you religious?" Stu nods his head affirmatively." Imagine Jesus in that group of people. Ask him, Do you love me? Let that grow. Is it a nice feeling?" Stu nods his head. "Now ask Jesus if he has any suggestions. Ask for three suggestions to help you get moving in a better and more productive direction. Tell me when you're done."

There is a fairly significant silence at this time before Stu Umped indicated he was ready.

"What were the three suggestions?" Gary asked.

Without hesitation, Stu shared: "Jesus said to love, live, and give; to live one day at a time; and to love my parents."

Gary spoke again. "Ok, you need to do one more thing to affirm that this experience real and not your imagination. Imagine Christ again, and let him know that you have had a tough life. What was his response?"

"Stu began to tear up. "God feels after me."

"He knows you, doesn't He? Now imagine yourself, but not you as you are now, but your eternal self, that part of you that existed before, exists now, and will exist after this life. I want you to complain to yourself. Say something like, 'Man, I've had a tough go.'"

Stu concentrated and then indicated, "My eternal self is smiling. He has a knowing smile of experience as he looks back at me."

"Think of Christ again, and ask him to hug you. Ask him to wrap you up in a bearhug and hold him tight. You know how you can feel and smell it. Just experience it. Can you feel it?" Gary paused. "Now ask Jesus one more thing: Will you still bring me home?" Pause. "What did he say?"

"Yes!"

Synopsis

When I was stumped working with Stu, I knew that change is an inside-out process. I also knew that we had covered themes similar to those that were uncovered in this imagery with Gary, but because of the unique nature of this session, Stu was able to find strength that came from the inside to make changes based on his values. There is a significant difference between talking about what is best and having an experience that realigns motivational and belief centers. It is not like Stewart never struggled again during his stay after this session, but he did find a center he could return to and a base to look back on that showed him he was loved, had purpose, and was worthy.

The overt Christian language was initially highly uncomfortable for me. One thing to be aware of is that you are not locked into the Christian iconography but can use the more ubiquitous terms of Higher Power. I keep a flexible menu of religious terminology. For example, I might say something like, "Imagine your Higher Power, Christ, Buddha, Vishnu, your eternal self, or whatever that looks like to you." I have found that almost universally the experience is more intense if there are the two layers of connection. First, people that have your best interest at heart; and second, a connection to a Higher Power. I have left the Higher Power portion out many times (especially early on in my attempt at utilizing these techniques) largely because of my own discomfort and fear of ethical implications. Yet, the experience is more productive, connecting, healing, and profound if both layers are included. I also feel that the menu model described allows for the client-centered approach that is necessary for this technique to be effective. The menu model alleviates the fear that we are telling them what to believe or what God is to them.

One of the cautions in using imagery is to provide our clients' room for the experience without dictating to them what it "should" look like or without superimposing our version of what the outcome should be. My goal is to open the door and guide the clients to their loved ones and Higher Powers, not to be central to the process.

Dee Thatch

Let me introduce you to another case study from my initial work with Dr. Weaver. Dee Thatch was adopted when he was eight years old by a loving couple that had tutored him while he was attending an inner-city school in a large urban area. They had felt strongly connected to him, and he had no one to really be involved in his life and look after him. He lived with an aunt, but she had several of her own children and cared for a few additional children from other relatives, and she was so spent and overwhelmed that Dee was practically a feral child. Over the years, several people he loved and respected had physically, emotionally, and sexually abused him. This was not known at the time of the adoption, but Dee Thatch had a highly fragmented mind, and he had learned to cope through disassociation. My assumption at the time was that some of the sexual abusive behaviors may also have a dissociative piece, based on his mother's description of catching him in the act one time and his responses being distant and distracted. Disassociation is a psychological protective device developed by resilient and strong people when placed in highly unsafe and irrational situations where the individual learns to check out and detach. Mentally Dee Thatch had likely developed this coping skill from a young age, and under stress it seemed to be his default cognitive state.

One of the struggles of working with trauma where disassociation is present is that the explicit memories are lost in the mind and are frequently difficult or impossible to recall. In treating the problem, sometimes the learning has to come while in a detached state, which is clearly complicated and difficult to facilitate. Dee had done great in the program in general. He was a model resident and showed little behavioral disturbances. Yet any attempts at engaging trauma work seemed to be of limited utility. He was initially resistant to the idea of working on his past, and I had been very careful to work on things only as he was ready. I was careful and respectful in making invitations to dig into some of the unresolved past issues. I didn't want to create a situation where there were power dynamics that mirrored abuse dynamics and by so doing traumatize or retraumatize him. Dee Thatch was preparing for transition out of the facility, and I had a gnawing fear that we had never sufficiently dealt with the dissociative piece.

As was my tendency when I felt stuck, I invited Gary to participate in a session. Gary was an old-school psychologist and had been trained in hypnosis, and I hoped that modality—in which I had no background—could create a safe detachment for Dee Thatch to do trauma work. After several years living with his new family, they had two biological children, and in time it came out that Dee had sexually abused them. To my surprise, Gary did not choose to use hypnosis but guided imagery as the preferred tool of intervention. The following is a transcript of the dialogue that was recorded in my supervision journal.

> Gary began the imagery work. "Imagine a group of people that have your best interest at heart, but your brother comes by invitation only. Ask this group of people, 'Do you love me?' When you think of your loved ones, who are the predominant persons who you see?"
> "My parents," Dee responded.
> "Which one is more vivid in your mind?"
> "Both."
> "Imagine them giving you a big hug. As you cling to them and they hold onto you, you are able to smell, hear, and touch them. As you are standing there, Christ approaches and wraps around you all. You are enveloped in a cocoon of love." In this moment, tears began to trickle down Dee's face. This is the first overt emotional reaction that I have witnessed with him in the ten months we had been working together. Gary continued speaking.
> "You now see your brother standing just outside this bubble of love. Can you see him?" Dee nods. "Make sure that you maintain the intensity of the cocoon of love that encompasses you, your folks, and Christ. When you feel secure, invite your brother to step into the bubble and feel the intensity of love that you can feel. Whose choice is it to make the step?
> "My brother's."

"Did he do it?" Dee nods. "If it is too uncomfortable for him, ask him to just taste it, and give him permission to step back."

"There was a drain when he stepped into the bubble," Dee remarked.

"That is ok. Can you feel the full power of the loving bubble once again?"

"Yes."

"Ok, then if you are ready, I want you to talk with your brother about the abuse and the impact it had on you. Let me know how it goes. You want to look for a way to resolve it so there is a place where we can all go to get healed."

There is a long gap of time at this point, probably around fifteen minutes, during which Dee Thatch has a slow stream of tears running down his face. I am not a particularly emotional person, but I find myself wiping tears off my cheek as I watch this brave young man battle these inner daemons. After some time, Gary continued.

"Carl Jung says we have a mask and a shadow. These cover who you really are. The real self becomes smaller as the mask and shadow become more defined and loom larger. I want you to create a homunculus. That is, I want you to create a little version of yourself that is the ugliest part of yourself. The homunculus takes on and represents your abusive behavior, that deepest darkest piece of yourself. What do you want to do with the homunculus?"

"Change it."

"Christ can see that shadow self. What is Christ doing with him?"

"Accepting him."

"One time I had a client that was working with this homunculus, and he described this experience of having energy from the bowels of Christ come out and wrap around his homunculus, and it slowly faded. Can you see it?" Dee nods. "When the energy came out, Christ groaned, but he still smiles. Did your family see it?" Dee nods again. "Do they still invite you into the cocoon of love?

"Ask Christ, 'Is something healed in my soul that I can let go of?'" Dee nods. "Watch your family. They have seen this dark shadow. Ask them, Do you still love me—less, same, more?"

"More."

Synopsis

Dee Thatch frequently quoted scripture and used biblical language. He talked a lot about prayer, God watching over him, and Christ as his friend. These were tools Dee felt empowered to use in his personal healing. Clients do not have to be as overtly religious as Dee in order to utilize this theme and introduce the concept of Divine assistance in healing, but in this case, it was an obvious and natural bridge. Dee took to the imagery format well and felt connected in part because it drew from his own Christ-based iconography.

I remember in my early work as a therapist intern, I had the opportunity to work with young victims of sexual crime. My clients ranged in age from three to twelve years old. As I was working with this population, I remember my supervisor encouraging me to help the kids break down their feelings of "loyalty" to the perpetrator and tap into the anger that comes from being victimized. The goal was not to create anger in the client but to provide a safe place for its expression.

In contrast to that early instruction, Gary never attempted tapping into anger; his imagery was solely based on this idea of safety and the "cocoon of love." That term alone is something I have adapted into my language just because it is so soothing. I asked Gary about this, and he simply told me, "Well, anger is one way to do it. But God is love, and healing comes from a loving place, and love is more powerful than anger, embarrassment, sadness, or whatever else comes up for someone." Gary's focus is on tapping into the loving place, and if these other emotions are stifled and need a place to manifest, there is nothing wrong with that, but it may not always be necessary to go through the feelings of anger in order to find healing.

One of the messages that fundamentally changed my way of thinking about clinical practice was Gary's undivided attention to approaching others with love. He was very emotionally intuitive and in tune with the healing power of love. As he worked through hard issues with clients, he would often have a slow drip of tears running down his face. He used to tell me that the only thing he has to offer clients is his time, love, and tears for their suffering. What a simple and powerful message.

Conclusion

When I ran across these transcripts, I felt it would be appropriate to have a snapshot of the intervention from the source from which I received it. As you can see, Gary is less rigid in his introductions to the imageries than I am. I don't know that one is better than the other. I do know that I am rigid in some ways, and I like to know the rules and parameters around things. The repetitious language you have been subjected to throughout the template chapters is simply to provide a foundation and language for those of us that want more than a vague invitation to be creative with guided imagery.

Neither of these sessions represent the best or most powerful change experiences I was able to witness Gary perform. Yet they do give you a sense of the principles that underlay the intervention. Gary often used playful interactions with clients including in the guided imagery itself.

I remember one intervention where he was doing an image with a young man that was tapping into the love of his grandmother who had passed, and Gary joked with the grandmother about how old they were and how he was going to join her on the other side of this life shortly. The young man would relay messages from his grandmother and Gary would respond, and everyone was belly-laughing as the interaction played out.

Gary's love for people and the work was contagious. I hope that some of that experience has rubbed off on you as you have explored these ideas and experiences with me. The final chapter is simply an invitation to go out and do the work. You have all the information that you need to be successful, and it is time to go and do. Change the world one person and one interaction at a time.

YOU CAN DO THIS!

Dawn

My intention throughout this book has been to show that guided imagery is a simple and effective tool, it has great flexibility and potentially limitless applications, and you can do this! To show that you can do this, I want to share a story of a few experiences I have had with others using this tool who have reported back to me about their experience.

Many years ago, I had the opportunity to present this material for the first time at a formal conference. I traveled to Irvine, California, to present for ninety minutes on Post-Materialist Guided Imagery and Trauma Resolution. It may be obvious, but I would like to dissect the title that I chose for that particular conference. Post-Materialist is simply detaching from things (wealth, property, material stuffs) in favor of ideals and something bigger than oneself. Spirituality is an example of such an ideal.

Spirituality in psychotherapy is not a widely practiced or discussed theme, despite the success of spiritual-based systems such as Alcoholics Anonymous. At the end of the day, Post-Materialist felt like a safer word than Spiritual or Divine, which was the underlying message I was trying to communicate. Guided Imagery is a bit more obvious and references the process of using the power of the mind to envision and imagine things. "Trauma" can be a controversial word these days as there are great divisions in the therapeutic world about what constitutes a trauma. I tend to separate trauma into two parts: big-T trauma and little-t trauma.

Big-T trauma consists of the major life events that present a fear of the loss of life or a violation of safety and personal space. Examples of big-T trauma could include a car accident, war, someone threatening you with a weapon, rape, or molestation. Little-t trauma would be experiences that may be less stark and singular but nevertheless leave intense emotional scars. Examples of little-t trauma could include parental divorce, bullying, intense embarrassment, or institutionalization.

The end of the title used the word "resolution." Resolution implies that there is a "solution" and that something can be fixed. This word was selected intentionally. A rational alternative might be to simply call it "therapy." It could become an acronym (PMGITT—post materialist guided imagery and trauma therapy) like so many therapy interventions, such as CBT, DBT, EMDR, ACT, TF-CBT, etc. Instead my goal was to offer the bold claim that trauma symptomology could be addressed in such a way that it could be fixed or resolved.

That claim may be overly optimistic. I have certainly engaged clients with guided imagery who continued to suffer and a resolution did not take hold. That stated, unlike other techniques I have used, guided imagery has aided in creating healing moments for my clients. Healing has transpired more often with this technique than any other tool in my therapeutic belt. I have seen immediate growth and at times complete cessation of trauma symptomology. But there are certainly instances where the imagery work seemed to be an unmistakable piece of the change experience, and yes, even full resolution.

I remember having grandiose visions of changing the world when I sallied into the conference in Irvine. I was convinced that this information was so important and revolutionary that it would take wings and become a thing in and of itself. Instead I had the experience that we often have after building up a specific moment. It was a fun presentation. There was good participation. I felt really good about it, and the audience seemed to come along for the ride and get a lot out of it. And then it was simply done. It was over. Nothing took off, the axis of earth did not shift, and a trauma healing revolution did not begin. We could not talk more overtly about experiences of the Divine in our therapeutic experience. And guided imagery did not sweep the earth with its effective path towards trauma resolution.

But there was one experience I will never forget that came out of that conference. About eighteen months after my presentation, I was attending another conference in the Lake of the Ozarks, Missouri. At conferences like this, practitioners try to gain favor with educational consultants (professionals who refer clients in private industry). As the clinical director of my program, it was my responsibility to do this political work.

You Can Do This!

I was at an opulent dinner with a few important educational consultants in a beautiful restaurant with glass walls that overlooked the lake. As the sun set, the color palate on the water was worthy of a master painter. During the course of the dinner, I was approached by a young therapist (we will call Jane) who wanted an opportunity to converse. Because I was otherwise occupied, I informed her that I would love to speak with her but was unavailable at the moment. I left Jane my card and told her she could call me, or if she felt inclined, we could speak after dinner.

I am not sure how long our meal went on after that, but it was at least an hour before we closed things up and were returning to the hotel for the night. As I left the restaurant, Jane was waiting in the foyer. I excused myself from the rest of the group and sat down to speak with her.

Jane told me that she felt compelled to share an experience that was born from a training she attended in Irvine California about eighteen months previously. She worked with young-adult women with Borderline Personality Disorder (BPD). Clients with BPD can be a challenge because of their intense emotional liability, interpersonal skill deficits, and propensity for self-harm and suicidality.

One of Jane's clients, who we will call Dawn, had completed the residential treatment program where Jane worked. A few months after completing treatment, Dawn called Jane in a moment of crisis. Jane had seen the emotional volatility and patterns of self-harm with Dawn early in treatment, but Dawn had stabilized enough to complete the program. But when Jane was taking this phone call, she sensed that something was inherently different this time. Jane had a gut instinct that Dawn was not really reaching out for help; she was calling to say goodbye. Jane was terrified that Dawn was going to hang up and kill herself.

Dawn lived in a different state than Jane. Dawn's parents could be alerted to Dawn's emotional state, but there was no way to know where Dawn was and how to get her help or if she could even be reached in time. Even more concerning was "if" someone could help. You can imagine the situation, being on the phone talking with a suicidal client, not having the ability to do anything to help.

In that moment Jane remembered a seminar on guided imagery. She shuffled through files in her desk and pulled out a handout. It was the same one-page document found at the beginning of chapter 5 of this book. The page had a picture of a therapist and client facing one another in chairs. Underneath was written, 1) Imagine a group of people that has your best interest at heart. Alive or dead, known or unknown, anyone throughout all humanity, but they must have this one common theme: your best interest at heart. 2) Ask that group of people, "Do you love me?" And feel the response! 3) Imagine that from among this group of people steps forward your Higher Power. 4) Connect with that entity and ask, "Do you love me?" And feel the response!

That was it. The beginning and the end of the instructions. Jane took the sheet and began to speak with Dawn. She told Dawn to close her eyes, to imagine a group of people, and to ask them if they loved her. Jane told Dawn to connect with the Divine and ask the same thing. Dawn engaged, and by the end of the conversation, she was calm, and Jane could feel peace from Dawn even through the distance of the phone. Dawn lived to see morning, and Jane attributed guided imagery to saving Dawn's life that night, over the phone, from a different state. This good caring therapist may have been able to work Dawn off the cliff without guided imagery, but it was a tool Jane had at a moment when she felt otherwise distressed and unprepared, and it worked.

Jane had minimal training, and she was able to save the life of a client and continue to help more. You already have more training from reading this book than she had in that ninety minute seminar; so you can do this too.

Ireful & Reece Iliant

My experience working with clients that have sexually offended on others has introduced me to the schizophrenic impact that such abuse can have on family systems where the abuser and the victim are intrafamilial. Parents struggle with the pull between being so mad at their child that offended, the need to nurture and support those that were victimized, and at the same time wanting to protect the child they are mad at for offending. There was a time I was working with a very distraught mother, we will call Ireful, and her son we will call Reece Ilient.

The set up was an unfortunately common experience in that particular setting. Reece was the oldest of four siblings. There were clear vestiges of love and care in his family, but there were also clear problems. Emotional abuse was fairly constant, and episodes of domestic violence between Reece Ilient's parents reinforced a fearful and unpredictable environment.

When Reece was fourteen, it was discovered he had been sexually abusing his younger siblings for more than a year. The sexual abuse was fairly extensive and frequent. The parents appropriately reported the abuse and sought help for all of the kids. Reece was placed in our residential facility, and the younger siblings began outpatient therapy.

Quarterly our facility would have "parent weekends" where we invited all the parents of residents to come out for three days of group therapy, classes, activities, and visits with their sons. One of the struggles in residential care is to maintain consistent contact with families. For that reason, the phone calls in the facility were virtually never restricted, even when they had difficult behavior. There were times that contact was restricted if the calls themselves seemed to consistently precipitate negative outbursts, but fostering communication and contact was generally the overriding need in the vast majority of situations.

During one of these parent weekends, we had panel discussion with only the parents. The panel consisted of therapists, administration, medical staff, line staff supervisors, and usually a boy or two. In these sessions, parents were given the opportunity to ask anything that they were interested in knowing, and we would respond to their questions. During this particular panel discussion, we had Ireful basically monopolizing the time. Taking all the time was one problem, but she also was venomous and attacking towards her son's therapist, which made the situation worse.

I remember trying to redirect some of the animosity by responding to questions that were challenges rather than informational, trying to refocusing the group away from the therapist who was clearly distraught and uncomfortable. Many of the mother's concerns seemed petty, and she would stack concerns without hearing responses. The panel was not a total loss, and with some juggling, we were able to have other parents participate without completely offending Ireful, but it was tense and not optimal.

I went home that night mulling over the interaction with Ireful. I can be a bit slow at times, but eventually my brain was able to piece a few things together. Although Reece was not my client, I made sure to run at least one group at all three of our facilities so that I always had a finger on the pulse of the group and each individual boy. I could not spend time doing individual therapy with everyone, but group dynamics give a personal and effective snapshot of how individuals within the group are functioning, progressing, or otherwise.

In addition to group I sat in all of the team meetings as we staffed boys, treatment issues/needs, and discussed the plan for helping each boy be successful. So, despite not being Reece's therapist I had a wealth of information and experiences to draw from. Reece was engaged and invested at this stage of his therapy. He was working hard and demonstrating a good understanding of the problems of the past, and he was developing skills and plans for being successful in the future.

Tension in the family had seemed to increase in proportion to his success. The family seemed eager to reinforce any negative feedback they heard about Reece and would quickly identify faults whenever positive reports were communicated. Part of their grievance with the program was that they wanted it to be focused on therapy and eliminate luxuries such as activities. They felt like the kids were being rewarded for their offending behavior.

While Reece Ilient was building relationships in the program, his younger siblings were having night terrors, and while he was learning self-care through coping skills, proper diet, exercise and calisthenics, his mother continued to struggle in the wake of his abusive actions back home.

This mother had split feelings. She was torn between wanting her son to be safe and improve and being frustrated and angry at the damage he had caused. She was overwhelmed with the responsibility of childcare. It did not seem "just" that Reece could be recovering and healing while those he victimized were suffering so much. The experience was overwhelming for her.

You Can Do This!

While contemplating this complicated situation I came to realize the underlying problem, and I had an uncomfortable solution present itself to my mind. I had the idea I should teach her how to do trauma imagery work. Now her children were receiving professional help from competent clinicians. Ireful is not a therapist. Teaching her a therapeutic tool seemed like an odd approach to a very serious problem.

The next day as I arrived at the facility, I ran into Ireful. I asked her if she would be willing to sit down with me and talk prior to the activities of the day. She consented and joined me in my office. I started by validating the confusing experience of Reece's success in treatment while she was stuck managing the nightmare at home. Then I offered to teach her guided imagery as a tool she may consider implementing with her children.

I spent about thirty minutes going over some of the underlying theory and principles that guide my thinking with imagery work and more specifically the trauma imagery template that was presented in chapter 6. After this interaction, we both returned to the festivities of the day. She was less disruptive throughout the remainder of the time at the facility, and I went on with the chaos of things and had eventually forgot about the exchange.

Several months later, Ireful called and followed-up with me on our conversation. Ireful described how she had returned to the home after the parent weekend, and that night one of the kids wet their bed and had a nightmare. She helped her little one clean up and prepared dry sheets. As she tucked the child in, she asked if the little one would be willing to try something. The mother then walked her child through a trauma imagery. Within a few days, she had taken opportunities to walk through the exercise with each of her kids.

According to her report, the trauma symptomology began to ameliorate. The nightmares disappeared and the toileting issues spontaneously remitted. Things were not perfect, and there was still emotional drama at times, but what had seemed overwhelming and unsolvable became manageable. Armed with a simple tool with minimal training, this mother was able to achieve the resolution to trauma in a way that had not happened up until that point.

Healing is a complex issue. These children were not immediately withdrawn from therapy but continued to benefit from those services. There is probably no such thing as a 'one and done' in healing. I think of these experiences more like creating a candle. You dip the wick over and over, and the wax collects thicker and thicker. The candle becomes more substantial and solid through the repetitious exposure to the hot wax and cooling process.

In a lot of ways treatment is like that. In this case the trauma intervention by this loving mother was probably timed in such a way that the candle gained an extra important coat. Resilience and healing were the end byproduct. I know I have said this before, but imagery is not the panacea. It will not fix all things all the time, but it is certainly something I have appreciated having access too as I have worked in this challenging and rewarding space of clinical intervention.

It has been said that the ultimate goal of a therapist is to work him or herself out of business. In an ideal world, my services would not be needed. There would be no sexual violence or assault. In a perfect world, all kids could stay in a loving and supportive home safely and not require residential placement. But until that time comes, I want to have as many tools as possible to foster healing. Guided imagery just happens to be my favorite tool. It represents less than 10% of the interventions I use, but when former clients call me years after leaving treatment, the two things they usually reminisce about are guided imagery and the therapeutic wilderness experiences we had together.

Confession

I would like to conclude with a confession. Despite having had many powerful and healing experiences with clients using imagery, I personally struggled to connect when it was done with me. Dr. Gary Weaver, my mentor, strongly believed that it was important to have a taste of the experience in order to shape and foster it with others. Therefore, he would periodically attempt to engage me in an imagery. I would close my eyes and imagine a group of people with my best interest at heart. And I would imagine my Higher Power. I would ask them, Do you love me? And I would attempt to feel the response.

Unfortunately, I am a good clinician but a bad client. I struggled to see the group in my mind's eye or to imagine connecting with the Divine. I use the tool because I saw the success that Gary had with my clients. I saw the change and the "proof was in the pudding," as they say. For years Gary supervised me on a weekly basis. We would talk theory, examples, and at times practice in supervision with clients in vivo.

Yet each time he would try to work his magic on me, I shut it out. I don't think I need to dive too deep into this confession to work on my own clinical issues around fear of connecting and my own walls that I struggled to even see at that time, but what I know is that although guided imagery seemed to work miracles with my clients, I just did not experience it personally. For me this is not a game killer, but it was just an oddity. Ironically, I had a similar experience during

EMDR basic training. Some of my psychological blocks seem to be thick.

Then one day Gary put me on assignment. He told me to have an imagery done to me by my wife. He recommended that I do an imagery with her so she could have the experience and get a feel for how it works and then have her do it to me.

This became a game changer. For whatever reason, when I did not feel the expectation and pressure to connect, I connected. My beautiful wife walked me through the steps, and for the first time, I did not overthink it. I did not try to analyze the process. I just let it happen.

Undoubtedly there was a foundation of trust that opened the doorway for my experience. It was a sweet and connecting experience. My wife and I began to experiment with one another using imagery work. This exercise was nurturing and loving and brought us closer in an intimate and emotional way that we probably had not previously felt.

As we experimented with guided imagery, we would get up in the wee hours of the morning (5 am or so) before our gaggle of little ones started to get up for the day, and we would explore through imagery. Some of the experiences were quite impactful. There were little things, like in one imagery I was speaking with my Eternal Self and was told to reach out to an old friend I had not spoken to in years. That day I called him, and he told me that he had made the decision to hit reset on his life and get rid of all his social media and his old phone number. That very day he was going to change his number. After that point, I would not have any way of getting in contact with him. As a result of that inspired interaction, I have been able to maintain an ongoing relationship with this great man and friend.

There was another time that I had the impression to reach out to a man I did not really even know all that well, that lived in my neighborhood. It turns out that very day he had been turned out of his house and his relationship with his wife was moving towards divorce. He talked about how hard it was, and we were able to share in his sorrow. It was like the Divine forces knew what he needed, and the imagery opened a conduit for communication that allowed me to play a small roll in comforting this man during his time of suffering.

My wife had a crazy experience during an imagery. She has always loved the kind and nurturing nature of Mother Teresa. My wife was invited in an imagery to speak with and interact with Mother Teresa in her mind's eye. My wife described the encounter by stating, at first they were talking, but then Mother Teresa asked my wife to walk with her through the streets of Calcutta. Mother Teresa explained that talking about compassion and suffering was insufficient. One must experience both, the darkness and the light. My amazing wife described walking hand in hand through the streets of Calcutta seeing with Mother Teresa's eyes and heart. My wife felt what mother Teresa felt and saw what she saw. My wife was left in tears and overwhelmed with a sense of love.

Conclusion

Gary used to tell me one of my greatest problems was that I shut the world off by living in my head. He was concerned that I discounted the importance and power of the heart. This book is a gift from my heart, intentionally separated from the fastidious intellectual part of myself. For those of you that are left brain leaning, like myself, I recognize this approach can be alienating. Just know it was not accidental.

If you have felt a spirit of love and healing in these pages, then I have communicated the essence of what I would

You Can Do This!

like you to know. I have intentionally chosen not to pursue an academic approach with this book. I love books with lots of reference material and citations for ideas. You will notice this book has only just touched on a few academic ideas and was not pursued with a more formal academic lens; but has been a collection of heart felt stories and simple templates.

I would love it if everyone reaching this point in the book has already experimented with the information that has been provided. I hope that you have already added your own stories to the ones I have shared through fostering a loving and healing environment with the people with whom you interact.

In the event that you have not ventured out into this new world of imagery that includes people with your best interest heart and Divine support, I recommend you do it now. Take the plunge. You have more than enough information to make it work. Thinking about it will not unleash the magic. Only by using it and sharing your experience will you fully unlock the potential of this peculiar gift.

Dr. Gary Weaver changed my life when he bestowed this gift upon me. I hope that it will now change your life. I hope that it changes the lives of those around you for the better. Now I bestow this gift upon you. Good luck, be creative, follow the intuitive tug, and unleash your full potential. Namaste.

Acknowledgments: I have been blessed with a supportive wife and family that have allowed me to dedicate time to my work and the healing of my clients. They have supported my desire to share my experience with others as I have completed the current project. I have benefited from the mentorship of many great clinicians and have been given creative license by my employers to work in the best interest of the clients that have had the courage to share their stories with me. I honor their courage and commitment to change and heal. I am also thankful to my editor, Alec Harding, who's suggestions and input was invaluable. I am grateful to my talented sister, Monica Stamm, who provided all of the artwork for the book. Finally, I am thankful to the Dr. Gary Weaver for his life and example and all that I have learned from him over the years. May he rest in peace.

BIBLIOGRAPHY

Anderson, H. (2010). *Hans Christian Andersen's Fairy Tails.* London: Puffin Books.

Brown, B. (2010). *The Gift of Imperfection: let go of who you think you are supposed to be and embrace who you are.* Minnesota: Hazeldon Publishing.

Carroll, L. (1865). *Alice's Adventures in Wonderland .* Sweden: London Macmillan & Co.

Delaney, H. M. (2007). Religiosity and Spirituality Among Psychologists: A Survey of Clinician Members of the American Psychological Association. *Professional Psychology and Research*, 38(5), 538-546.

Gilbert, E. (2006). *Eat, Pray, Love: One Woman's Search for Everything Across Italy, India, and Indonesia.* Santa Ana: Penguin Press.

Harlow H. F., D. R. (1965). Total social isolation in monkeys. *Proceedings of the National Academy of Sciences of the United States of America.*

Harris, N. (2014). How childhood trauma affects health across a lifetime. *TedMed,* (p. https://www.ted.com/talks/nadine_burke_harris_ho w_childhood_trauma_affects_health_across_a_lifeti me).

Jones, M. (2010). *Unreasonable Possibilities.* Wisdom House Books.

Jung, C. (1964). *Man and His Symbols.* Dell Publishing.

Lewis, M. (2015). *The Biology of Desire: why addiction is not a disease.* Public Afairs.

Longo, R. P. (2005). *Current Perspectives: Working with Sexually Aggressive Youth and Youth with Sexual Behavior Problems.* Holyoke: NERI Press.

N/A. (1939). *Alcoholics Anonymous.* Alcoholics Anonymous World Services.

Nietzsche, F. (1910). *The Joyful Wisdom.* Edinburgh: T.N. Foulis.

Shaw, J. (2016). *The Memory Illusion: Remembering, Forgetting, and the Science of False Memory.* London: Random House Books.

Shaw, J. P. (2015). Constructing Rich False Memories of Committing Crime. *Psychological Science*, 26(3).

Siegel, D. J. (2003). *Parenting from the inside out.* Penguin Group.

Skinner, J. (1998). *The Confession of St. Patrick.* Dell Publishing.

Trainum, J. L. (2016). *How the Police Generate False Confessions: an inside look at the interogation room.* Maryland: Rowman & Littlefield Publishing Group.

Tronick, E. A. (1975). Infant emotions in normal and pertubated interactions. *Paper presented at the biennial meeting of the Society for Research in Child Development.* Denver.